The Gospel
in Solentiname

The Gospel in Solentiname

Volume III

Ernesto Cardenal

Translated by Donald D. Walsh

ORBIS BOOKS
Maryknoll, New York 10545

Third Printing, October 1985

Originally published as *El evangelio en Solentiname*, vol. 2, pp.
1–155, copyright © 1977 by Ediciones Sígueme, Salamanca, Spain

English translation copyright © 1979 by Orbis Books,
Maryknoll, New York 10545

Orbis paperback edition 1982

Manufactured in the United States of America

Library of Congress Cataloging in Publication Data

Cardenal, Ernesto.
    The Gospel in Solentiname.

    Translation of El Evangelio en Solentiname.
    Dialogues on the Gospels between the author and community
members of Solentiname.
    1. Bible. N.T. Gospels—Criticism, interpretation, etc.—
Miscellanea.   I. Title.
BS2555.2.C27713 1976   226'.06   76-2681
ISBN 0-88344-174-8 (v.3)

CONTENTS

INTRODUCTION

In Solentiname, a remote archipelago on Lake Nicaragua with a population of *campesinos,*[1] instead of a sermon each Sunday on the Gospel reading, we would have a dialogue. The commentaries of the *campesinos* are usually of greater profundity than that of many theologians, but of a simplicity like that of the Gospel itself. This is not surprising: The *Gospel,* or "Good News" (to the poor), was written for them, and by people like them.

Some friends urged me not to let these commentaries be lost, but to put them together and publish them as a book. That's the reason for this book. I first began collecting them in my mind, insofar as I could. Later, with more common sense, we used a tape recorder.

Many of these commentaries were made in the church, at Sunday Mass. Others were made in a thatched hut opposite the church, used for meetings and the communal lunch after Mass. Occasionally, we would have the Mass and the Gospel dialogue in the open air on other islands, or in a small house that we could get to by rowing along a beautiful river through very tropical vegetation.

Each Sunday we first would distribute copies of the Gospels to those who could read. There were some who couldn't, especially among the elderly and those who lived on islands far away from the school. One of those who could read best (generally a boy or a girl) would read aloud the entire passage on which we were going to comment. Then we discussed it verse by verse.

We used the Protestant translation entitled *Dios llega al hombre,* which is the best translation of the Gospels that I know. The translation is anonymous, but it was unquestionably made by a poet. It is in the simple language of the Latin American *campesino,* but it preserves a maximum fidelity to the Scriptures.[2]

I'm sorry I can't include the many good dialogues we had before we began to collect them—they were carried off by the wind of the lake—nor some others we had when our tape recorder had broken down. But these dialogues have been lost only for this book, not for those who took part in them and who in some way retain them even though they may not remember them.

The archipelago of Solentiname has thirty-eight islands; some are very small, and only the largest are inhabited. The population is about a thousand, composed of some ninety families. The houses are usually thatched huts, all spread out, some distance apart, on the shores of the different islands. On one point of the largest island we established our little community or lay monastery, Our Lady of Solentiname. To this community came the Colombian poet William Agudelo and his wife, Teresita, and their two small children, Irene and Juan; and also some young people born on these islands: Alejandro, Elvis, and Laureano. Communication with the outside was infrequent, and our contemplative retirement was not disturbed in this place, fortunately hard to reach, outside the paths of merchants and tourists.

Not all those who lived on these islands came to Mass, many because they had no boat, and others because they missed the devotion to the saints, to which they were accustomed. Others stayed away through the influence of anti-Communist propaganda, and perhaps also through fear.

Not all those who did come took an equal part in the commentaries. There were some who spoke more often. Marcelino is a mystic. Olivia is more theological. Rebeca, Marcelino's wife, always stresses love. Laureano refers everything to the Revolution. Elvis always thinks of the perfect society of the future. Felipe, another young man, is very conscious of the proletarian struggle. Old Tomás Peña, his father, doesn't know how to read, but he talks with great wisdom. Alejandro, Olivia's son, is a young leader, and his commentaries are usually directed toward everyone, and especially toward other young people. Pancho is a conservative. Julio Mairena is a great defender of equality. His brother Oscar always talks about unity. The authors of this book are these people and all the others who talk frequently and say important things, and those who talk infrequently but also say something important, and with them William and Teresita and other companions that we have had and who have taken part in the dialogues.

I am wrong. The true author is the Spirit that has inspired these commentaries (the Solentiname *campesinos* know very well that it is the Spirit who makes them speak) and that it was the Spirit who inspired the Gospels. The Holy Spirit, who is the spirit of God instilled in the community, and whom Oscar would call

the spirit of community unity, and Alejandro the spirit
of service to others, and Elvis the spirit of the society
of the future, and Felipe the spirit of proletarian struggle, and Julio the spirit of equality and the community
of wealth, and Laureano the spirit of the Revolution,
and Rebeca the spirit of Love.

NOTES

1. *Campesino* is literally one who lives in the *campo* (country,
field). Most *campesinos* are farm workers, but some are
fisherfolk.—D.D.W.

2. The Gospel quotations in this edition are my translations from
the Spanish of *Dios llega al hombre.*—D.D.W.

1.

The Transfiguration

(Luke 9:28–36)

And while Jesus was praying,
his face changed in appearance,
and his clothes became white and shining.

OLIVIA: "That change happened to him so
the disciples would see he was going to rise
from the grave, and so we can see we're going
to be transformed like him. If we change our
attitude we're going to have the same change
his face and his clothes had. That light they
saw in him will be in us too."

MARIA: "This happened when he was praying. And I think that for us too it's important
to pray. He was praying to prepare himself for
what he was going to suffer."

There appeared two men conversing with
him,
who were Moses and Elijah, surrounded by a
glorious splendor,

1

*and they were talking of the death that Jesus
was going to suffer in Jerusalem.*

TOMAS: "And those two dead men that appear beside him and that are very happy, it's to make us see they hadn't died, and they were not only alive, they had a better life."

FELIPE, Tomás's son: "That was also to give them courage, because Jesus was going to be like the two of them, but only after suffering the same death that they did. And that's why they're talking about his death."

They asked me why Moses and Elijah appeared, and I said that Moses was the great liberator of the people, that he brought them out of Egyptian slavery, and Elijah was a great prophet, a defender of the poor and the oppressed, when Israel again fell into slavery, with social classes. Both of them were closely identified with the Messiah, for it had been said that the Messiah would be a second Moses and that Elijah would come back to earth to denounce injustices as a precursor of the Messiah (and Jesus said that Elijah had already arrived in the person of John the Baptist).

WILLIAM: "They're talking about his death, and they're in glory too, sharing that glory of his. It seems to me it's because all people who share the sufferings of Christ and struggle for his cause (for freedom) will share in that same glory of his, like those two prophets. And I believe that when they were talking about his death they weren't talking just about him but also about all people who together with him were going to enjoy that same happy ending."

OLIVIA: "As I see it, the resurrection is something you can already begin to have in this life. Christ was still made of mortal flesh, and they already see him with that brightness, that light so beautiful, the way he'd be after his death, resurrected. The others hadn't seen this, only these disciples had this vision. They've seen Jesus this way, already transfigured in life because of the death he was going to have. And what they saw there you can apply to the people, the people still suffering. They're transfigured like Christ even though we can't see it, because the people are Christ himself."

ELVIS: "There's two kinds of death: the death of somebody who isn't united to the people that's Christ, and that's a real death; and then there's the death of somebody who *is* united, and that's a death with resurrection."

WILLIAM: "It seems to me the victory over death is when somebody, because of the good he's done for others, becomes part of future humanity, which will be resurrected. Even though your death is obscure and nobody remembers it, you stay alive in the consciousness of humanity. And what the disciples saw in that little moment is the glory of that future humanity."

I: "The translation that we have read says they were talking about 'his death,' but Saint Luke is really saying that they were talking about 'his departure,' and this is interesting because in Greek 'departure' is called Exodus, and this is the word that he uses. And by this he's saying too that with his death Jesus was going to head a new Exodus, a new departure of the people toward freedom. We can read the text as if it literally said, 'They were talking of the departure of Jesus.' "

FELIPE: "The Exodus is the revolution."

I: "In the Bible, God appears fundamentally 'ike the God of Exodus, which is like saying the God of freedom. The prophet Amos says that the Exodus of Israel was not the only one and that Yahweh had brought other peoples out of other slaveries. Which is like saying that Yahweh is the God of every revolution."

REBECA: "That Jesus, he's here now in this community freeing us from all slavery. We can see him shining in the unity of the community, with the light they saw in him, which is the light of love."

OSCAR: "If we don't sleep through it."

*Although Peter and his companions were
    very sleepy
they stayed awake and they saw the glory of
    Jesus
and the two men who were with him.*

OLIVIA: "The Passion was near, and maybe those two were there to give him courage and strengthen him in his decision to die for the freedom of humankind."

WILLIAM, smiling: "They must have talked and talked there that night, because the apostles were so sleepy."

When those men were going away from Jesus,
Peter said to him:
"Master, what a good thing we're here!
Let's build three huts:
one for you,
another for Moses,
and another for Elijah."
But he didn't know what he was saying.

LAUREANO: "He was confused."

OSCAR: "He has a vision of heaven and he wanted to stay there, without having to suffer. He wanted heaven but without suffering, he wanted it free for nothing, without stewing, and that's what's wrong with me too."

OLIVIA: "A little while before that, Peter had told Jesus they shouldn't go to Jerusalem on any account, and now we see that he's very pleased there enjoying the joy of the resurrection without suffering. He thought that was all they had to do, just be there sitting pretty, without having to struggle. He didn't know what he was saying, because he thought they could stay like that, without suffering. He didn't know it was a vision and that they had to come back to reality. That glory was real, but it was in the future and it would be the result of suffering."

MARIITA: "That vision was to struggle."

And while they were talking, a cloud came
*   and covered them,*
and they were afraid when they saw them-
*   selves inside the cloud.*

> *Then inside the cloud a voice was heard say*
> *ing:*
> *"This is my beloved Son; listen to him."*

FELIPE: "They weren't very socially conscious and that's why they were scared."

I: "In the Bible the cloud is an image of the presence of God. He accompanied the people during the Exodus in the shape of a cloud. In the Sinai he appeared surrounded by clouds And when the temple of Jerusalem was inaugurated, it is said that his presence filled the temple like a mist. And that's also why the Gospel says that Jesus in his ascension was enveloped in a cloud. The cloud is something that you see and that prevents you from seeing. That's why it's the image of God, which is revealed to us and at the same time is hidden from us. Or rather it's revealed to us as a mystery; its presence is an emptiness, and its being is a void to the senses. What is said in this passage is that they were enveloped by the mystery of God."

REBECA: "They were scared because that thing enveloped them, but they shouldn't have been scared because they were being enveloped by a loving God, who was saying that Jesus was his beloved Son and that they should listen to him because he was going to talk to them about love."

I: "Christ is the word of God made flesh on earth, the message of God that we should love one another. That's the word that the cloud says we must hear."

OSCAR: "We must hear it and obey it."

MARCELINO: "Here we too are enveloped in that cloud of God telling us to listen to Jesus, not listen to God, because he doesn't talk to us directly. He talks to us through Jesus. With that word, which is love, we're going to be transfigured like him, when all of humanity is unified, and we're going to transfigure the world, because even his clothes were filled with light."

After the voice spoke, they saw that Jesus was
*   alone.*
They kept silent,
and they said nothing to anyone about what
*   they had seen.*

LAUREANO: "Because if they told it the others would think they were crazy."

WILLIAM: "I believe it was for the same reason that he told them earlier, when they spoke of the Messiah: 'Do not say that I am the Messiah.' It was a secret they had to keep because of the repression."

I: "Yes, first they found out that he was the Messiah; afterwards he revealed to them that as the Messiah he had to suffer and die; now he makes them see that through his death he would have a glorious transformation and all this was the same messianic secret that they had to keep. They would tell it after the resurrection."

OLIVIA: "And maybe they wouldn't understand it till then. Because when Jesus told them he had to suffer they didn't understand him, and the glory of Jesus they saw here was the glory of his suffering and death."

Young IVAN, Olivia's son: "Maybe they fell asleep and dreamed all this."

I: "It seems that this whole story is purely symbolical. The mountain talked about here wouldn't be any mountain in Palestine. It's a new Sinai where God, by means of a new Moses, gives a new law, the law of love. Peter talks about building some huts or tents because the prophets had said that, with the Messiah, God would live again in a tent in the midst of his people, as in the Exodus. We've already read in the Prologue to the Gospel of Saint John that, with Christ, God 'planted his tent in the midst of us.' Peter 'didn't know what he was saying' because they couldn't stay there, they had to begin the new Exodus toward liberty."

MARCELINO: "This community is already on the move, and God is in the midst of our huts."

2.

"He Who Is Not Against Us Is with Us"

(Luke 9:49–50)

Then John said to him:
"Master, we have seen one who in your name
*   cast out evil spirits;*
and we forbade him,
because he was not one of us."
But Jesus said to him:
"Do not forbid him:
for he who is not against us is with us."

ALEJO: "That's very timely, because there are so many people now who aren't Christians, or don't call themselves Christians, and they do great social work, make great revolutions, you might say great miracles. And over and over again they've told us Christians not to have anything to do with them. Here Christ tells us that anyone that works for the cause of others is on the side of us Christians."

His mother: "The ones that didn't have

9

Christian spirit were the disciples, who rejected that person who was doing very good things."

I: "This Gospel tells us that a person's not being a Christian doesn't matter: that person can be with us also; because our cause is the cause of humanity."

WILLIAM: "While there are others who are really against us. And there are some who try to pass themselves off as disciples of Christ and do evil to and exploit their neighbor; and there are others who, without calling themselves disciples, do good."

Another one: "And there are some too who confuse the issue by doing good. Like that spy from Security, disguised as a schoolteacher who was doing social things with the help of Caritas, and we had to prevent him from going on doing stupid things. That guy, passing himself off as a Christian, was doing harm, and we had to stop him, and we did. It's the opposite of the one in the Gospel who was doing good without being a disciple of Jesus."

FELIPE: "That man was a Christian because he cast out devils in the name of Jesus, and so he was a disciple."

I: "He wasn't a disciple, for John has told Jesus he wasn't a disciple, and that's why they forbade him."

ELVIS: "He didn't belong to the group, but he was doing the things that Jesus was doing, which is what's important."

MARCELINO: "Of course he believed in Jesus, because he used the name of Jesus."

LAUREANO: "And I believe he was really a disciple of Jesus that was going around there by himself, and the other disciples didn't know he was a disciple, but Jesus knew. And just because he was a disciple of Jesus he worked miracles. I believe there are right now people like that, and the Christians don't know that those people are disciples of Jesus too."

PANCHO: "Communists? They don't use Jesus' name."

LAUREANO: "They use the name of freedom, which is the same thing."

PANCHO: "They're against Jesus."

LAUREANO: "If they're not against the poor, they're not against Jesus. They're not against us."

OLIVIA: "What I'd like to know is why those disciples of Jesus were against that man who was doing good. Maybe just because he wasn't in a church crossing himself. But he was working against evil, he was casting out the devil. There's only evil and good, and he was doing good, so that means he was on the side of Jesus. I don't see why the others were against him, simply because the man wasn't an apostle."

TOMAS PEÑA, turning to me: "The first word by him that you read in the Book? Say it. . . . That's the one I want to talk about."

I read: "Do not forbid him: for he who is not against us is with us."

TOMAS: "That's what I was going to tell you, that what he was doing was correct. He's with us, or really with the whole community. Be-

cause Jesus is with us: he's with the whole
community. So he was doing the right thing,
like it says there. If you're with the community you're with God too, you're not for evil,
don't you think? And everybody who's not
doing evil is in favor of us."

A cousin of the Guevaras, who has come to
visit them: "And how did it happen he wasn't
with Jesus, he hadn't wanted to become a disciple of his? This is a legitimate question."

I: "Who knows, he probably had his reasons,
and Jesus respects those reasons."

TOMAS: "You could also say that that man
who, without being a Christian, is driving out
the devil, the devils, is showing us that any one
of us can do the same, having the right faith in
God."

LAUREANO: "Having it or even not having
it."

FELIPE: "Communion with people, that's
being with Jesus, and not having exploitation
among people (or among ourselves, the apostles; let us apostles not exploit each other
either).

I: "It's possible that that man was caring for
a sick man. The Gospel doesn't make much
distinction between being possessed by the
devil and illnesses; there's the case of a be-
devilled man that Saint Matthew calls 'epilep-
tic'; and there's the case of a hunchbacked
woman of whom Jesus says that she had been
'tied by Satan.' And how is it that he was curing in the name of Jesus? I think he was simply
doing what Jesus was doing."

ELVIS: "And Jesus doesn't divide men into people who are Christians and people who aren't. People who are driving out the devil, people who are driving evil out of the world: those are the people who are on our side, the people who are on the side of our community."

ALEJANDRO: "And Jesus here presents his church as very extensive."

3.

Nicodemus Visits Jesus

(John 3:1–21)

A group of us from Solentiname went to celebrate Mass in a settlement on the opposite shore, reached by going up the Papaturro River. The humble little church is in the middle of a cacao grove, and we discussed the Gospel while a strong wind shook the cacao trees. Some monkeys howled in the distance.

We read that a Pharisee called Nicodemus, who was an "important man," went at night to visit Jesus. Jesus said to him:

> *To tell the truth, he who is not born again*
> *cannot see the kingdom of God.*
> *Nicodemus asked him:*
> *"But how is it possible*
> *that an already grown man can be born*
> *again?*
> *Can he perhaps enter his mother again to be*
> *born again?"*

I said it appeared that this was a secret interview.

A *campesino* from Papaturro: "Since he was a Pharisee and an important man, maybe he was afraid to be seen with Jesus."

OLIVIA: "He needed to put aside hypocrisy and become converted to love. The Pharisees had a religion without love. Nicodemus can't understand how you can be born again: it's when a new consciousness is created in you; then you become a new person."

"A change of life; since it's a new life he calls it a new birth."

ELVIS: "It's the change from selfishness to love, and from a society based on selfishness to a society based on love, which means the kingdom of God. For a new society we need a new humanity, like born again. Only somebody who's been transformed, somebody new, can enter the kingdom."

JULIO: "To be born again is to be like a child. For the child there isn't any black or white, everything's alike, we're all equal. Among grown-ups, the rich never go to sit with the poor: the rich over there and the poor over here. That kingdom is the kingdom of equality, and to enter it we adults have to be like children again, we have to be born again."

NATALIA, the village midwife: "When you were born you were born innocent, right? You don't know anything evil. Then when you reach a certain age you pick up every evil thing. That's why when you become good it's like you were born again from your mother's womb. That old and very important man was very different from the way he'd been born."

OLIVIA: "It seems to me that to be born again

is to live in a community of love. We can be poor and selfish, and not have love for others or solidarity, and then we belong to the old society. If we live in unity, it's because we've been born again. If we're not united it's because we're not reborn, we go on being the same."

OSCAR: "Man, I was just thinking here that you're born from your mother; but you've got to be born again to enter into the kingdom. You're born and you come out innocent of everything, but the kingdom of God is a different society, with different people. And it seems to me baptism is so we'll be born again, right?"

And Jesus answered him:
"To tell the truth,
Anyone who is not born of water and the
    spirit
cannot enter the kingdom of God."

"It means that birth is more of the spirit than of anything else. Because the first birth is a birth of the flesh. The second one is more important because it's so that we can become good, receive the spirit."

OSCAR: "The spirit must come to you besides being bathed with the water, like when Jesus got baptized the spirit came through the air. Then that baptism with the water and the spirit is the same as Jesus', it seems to me."

I: "It's receiving the spirit of God."

OSCAR: "Right."

"Water washes, but baptism must wash us

with the spirit of love, a spirit that will purify us of the spirit of selfishness."

JULIO: "I understand that the baptism that Jesus talks about is a washing away of all the filth in people, all injustice, so we won't have a selfish society. A change of mind, then."

I: "John the Baptist had said he was baptizing with water (a mere ritual) but that Jesus would baptize with the Holy Spirit. The Holy Spirit is the spirit of God, which means love. At the end of this Mass we're going to baptize some children and that's why we have this water here, but we haven't come to carry out a mere ritual but to incorporate these children into a community so that they may receive the spirit of love."

GLORIA: "Religion by itself, like the Pharisees' religion, doesn't change society. It doesn't end injustices, exploitation. Christ is telling this Nicodemus (who was a Pharisee) that we must renew ourselves in love, which is the same as being born in the spirit, and which is the same as making ourselves new people. That's the only way we can create a new society."

> *"What is born of the flesh is flesh;*
> *what is born of the Spirit is spirit.*
> *Do not be surprised that I say to you:*
> *'Everyone must be born again.'"*

OSCAR: "As I understand it, it's clear to us all right now, anybody can feel it, we're seeing here that we're illuminated by the Holy Spirit. We're saying things that are very important, and you realize that it's the Spirit that's coming into you."

WILLIAM: "The Spirit of God that has been given to us, and that makes us transmit to others that Spirit."

"As I see it, this man had his religion but it was a very backward religion. And Christ tells him that those rituals are something purely human, 'what is born of the flesh is flesh,' and that that can't change the world. Only love can change the world. That's why they have to be born again, from the Spirit, which means from love."

WILLIAM: "And Jesus makes a distinction between the flesh and the spirit; the flesh dies but the spirit doesn't die, the spirit is what gives life to the flesh. 'And what is born of the Spirit is spirit': the new man, born of the Spirit, doesn't die either."

I added that, in fact, in the Bible spirit and life are the same thing. Jesus elsewhere, in the same Gospel according to Saint John, says that "the Spirit is the one that gives life, and the body by itself is useless."

> *The wind blows where it wishes;*
> *you hear the noise that it makes,*
> *but you do not know where it comes from or*
>   *where it goes.*
> *So also are all those who are born of the*
>   *Spirit.*

I said that in Hebrew, as also in Greek, the same word is used to say "wind" and "spirit."

The spirit was the breath of life and they imagined it like air. And here Jesus is playing with the two meanings of the same word. I said too that in the Bible the spirit of God or the Holy Spirit is the breath of God instilled in us. God blew that spirit into the first man, giving life to him. Every liberating action of God in history appears as if caused by that spirit (the urge for freedom that is in humankind). That is what moved the prophets to denounce injustice and oppression. And it seemed to me that Oscar was right when he said that spirit is the one that we're hearing talking here. That's the wind we hear but we don't know where it comes from, and it blows where it wishes.

OSCAR: "The way I see it, the Spirit is like that, like the wind, we just hear it. We don't know where the Spirit's born, where it comes from, or where it's going to wind up from now on. It's invisible, but we're feeling it like we feel the wind. In every answer we give when we're discussing the Bible we're feeling it. We speak through the Spirit, not through the flesh, for we're not educated or important people. This wind is love too, the spirit is love, and that's what makes us speak here, and we don't know where it comes from. It's speaking through us. I don't know how to explain it."

I: "Why, you've explained it very well. The Spirit is speaking through you. It blows where it wishes, and now it has chosen to blow here in this humble village of Papaturro."

OLIVIA: "I think it's also compared with the wind because the wind goes far, far away, so swift, for it goes thousands of miles, and it's like the spirit carrying the word of God, it goes invisible like the wind that goes wherever it wants, to the desert, to the mountain, wherever they want to listen to it and understand it. It goes traveling like a wind, like the wind that goes without stopping."

"This wind that's blowing here maybe comes from Solentiname, and who knows where it got there from," said JULIO, while we heard the strong wind shaking the cacao trees.

I: "It's come from very far away, this wind that we're feeling here and Jesus too says we don't know where it's going."

OSCAR: "It's endless. Because just as it blew here, it'll go and blow wherever it wants and it always keeps going."

WILLIAM: "It keeps going in history changing humanity and we don't know how far that change is going to get to in the future."

"The Spirit is love, which is among us, and it's changing the world; you can feel it, but it's mysterious. And what's born from this Spirit, the new person, is free like the wind is free. The Pharisees weren't free; they were enslaved by their laws and their religious rules. Jesus is telling them to get rid of those traditions and be free like the wind that blows wherever it wants to."

Then Nicodemus asked him again:
"How can this be?"
Jesus answered him:
"You who are a great teacher in Israel,

you don't know these things?
I tell you the truth, we speak of what we know
and we are witnesses of what we have seen;
but you all do not believe what we tell you.
If you do not believe me when I talk to you
  about the things of this world,
how are you going to believe me if I talk to
  you about the things of heaven?"

I said it seemed as though Jesus was speaking to him with a certain irony. It's as if he said to him: "You who are a doctor of theology."

OLIVIA: "And in spite of what Jesus said we still go on with the same religion of not eating meat on Friday, and if they kill some poor guy somewhere, who cares! They see that the candles are lighted to say the rosary. But if the people are going hungry, that's the will of God! And that's why Christ was telling them things couldn't go on like that. It's better to fight against injustice and not keep on with that false religion, all that praying and shouting, the way we used to have it and many people still have it in many places. A bunch of people fasting with hard hearts."

I: "And it seems that Jesus is saying to Nicodemus: 'We are speaking of the injustices that we have seen, of which we are witnesses, and you don't believe us.' "

"It seems *that* man was, as we say, a Somoza follower."

I: "Why?"

"Well, wasn't he an important guy there in Israel?"

I: "Jesus says that if they don't believe him when he talks to them about the things of this world, things that they're seeing every day, how would they believe him if he talked to them about the things of heaven? So Jesus is talking about the things of the earth, about the change he wanted here on earth, of the new birth here. He's not talking about heaven, because that would be useless and they wouldn't even understand him."

OSCAR: "I see it this way: This guy was important, he was with the others of his own class, and he was defending injustice. And when Jesus speaks to him about that injustice that everybody can see, he makes out he doesn't understand. And he asks and asks, and he was clinging to his religion, a kind of false religion, and that's why he doesn't understand him."

TERESITA, William's wife: "With simple people Jesus didn't have that problem. This man who's very educated is asking him a lot of questions because he doesn't understand him."

OSCAR: "Hell, it's just like now: some bastard is exploiting people, and somebody comes up to tell him he shouldn't do that. He makes out he doesn't understand and so he asks thousands of questions. That's the way that bastard seems to me."

No one has risen to heaven except the one who came down from heaven,
that is to say, the Son of Man, who is in heaven.

ALEJANDRO: "He tells him nobody can talk about heaven if he hasn't gone up there. There's not a single one who's gone up, there's only one who's come down, and he's the only one who can tell how it is."

OLIVIA: "And that's a nice phrase of Jesus', right? We really want to be saved by doing crazy things, far from God's commandment, to love our neighbor like ourselves, which we don't like. And we do a lot of things that God doesn't ask us to do, many religious duties but not what he asks. That's why that's nice, that phrase that nobody's been in heaven except him; and he's not talking about the things of heaven, he's talking about loving his neighbor right here on earth."

I: "So it seems that Jesus is telling him that just because of their religious concerns (about heaven) they don't understand things of the earth, how to change the world here. The only one who knows about the things of heaven is Jesus, and what he's talking about is a change on earth, and that's why he came down."

OSCAR: "So we refuse to understand what the world is. If we're going to be asking questions, what's up there, in heaven, the thing's a mess. I'm all mixed up."

I: "And maybe he wanted to get out of it, right?"

*And just as Moses raised up the serpent in
the desert,
the Son of Man must also be raised up,
so that everyone who believes in him will not
perish, but will have eternal life.*

I explained that when the serpents were biting the Israelites in the desert, Moses raised up a bronze serpent, and anyone who looked at it was cured.

"Man, it seems to me you can apply this to our people who are suffering from hunger and from the exploitation of the rich, and you see it's like a serpent biting you. It seems to me if you see the things that are going on and you understand how oppressed you are, you can get free. Jesus says it's him you have to look to because he's the victim of the injustices and sin. Seeing him, the people are watching their own oppression, the serpent that's biting them. I don't know if what I'm saying makes any sense but that's what came to my mind."

I said that what he had said seemed very sensible to me, and I added that in the Gospel according to Saint John "eternal life" doesn't mean life in heaven (Jesus is saying here that he's not talking about the things of heaven) but a life you can lead now here on earth. John himself says in one of his letters: "I have written to you so that you will realize that you have eternal life," although it's a life that presupposes also a triumph over death.

A *campesino* from the village: "It looks like we have to get involved in politics, but it seems to me that our politics ought to be the politics of the Son of God."

JULIO: "So anybody who's not political is not a Christian. We ought to fight for the common good, the good of everybody."

"Not like the politicians that govern us now,

that if we take just a tiny step to one side, they screw us."

I: "The politics of the Bible is the communion of all, with all things in common, and for that we need this new birth. We must cast off the old (the people of the old society), says Saint Paul, and clothe ourselves in the new, with no distinctions between Jew and Greek, masters and slaves. Che also used to talk a lot about this new person, the one for others; the one of the society of the future. He will have very different characteristics, he says, he's already being born, but his image isn't finished yet, and it can't be. And Che himself in his life clothed himself quite a bit in this new image."

OSCAR: "There's no point in talking about heaven, wanting now to go up to heaven to see what kind of a place it is; I think we've got enough on our hands to see what kind of a place the earth is."

OLIVIA: "I believe the things of the earth are the same as the things of heaven."

"Well, when people love each other there's a community of love, and that's heaven: where there's no divisions, no selfishness, where there's no deceit, that's where heaven is, that *is* heaven, that's glory."

"It's more joyful. It's a way of changing life and making it better."

OSCAR: "If we begin to be in love we already know heaven because that's where it comes from."

I: "What Olivia says is very good, that the things of earth are the same as the things of heaven, for we see that Jesus, who came down from heaven as it says here and who 'is in heaven,' didn't come to talk about anything different from the things of earth."

OSCAR: "Ernesto, that means that we're getting to know heaven, right? Because those bastards lived on earth and didn't know what there was on earth, they didn't see the evil. Everything bad they took for good, they were hypocrites, right? And now there's been progress and many of us now know what heaven is, what's earth and what's heaven."

I: "We're receiving that spirit that blows where it wishes, and we don't know where it comes from. Well, it comes from heaven."

> *For God loved the world so much*
> *that he gave his only Son,*
> *so that everyone who believes in him*
> *will not perish but have eternal life.*

FELIPE: "It seems to me, then, that to believe in Jesus is to believe in love. It seems to me that if you have faith but don't have love, it's no good, you have to believe in love."

WILLIAM: "And it's clear that it's a faith accompanied by action. Those who believe in him work and therefore don't perish; they work so that they won't perish and so that others won't perish. Love and eternal life are the same. Those who believe in him are the ones who practice justice and love, and therefore they have that life."

I: "It seems to me that humanity is a complete organism, a single body, and it has eternal life. But only the individuals who are united with humanity, those who love, share in the life of this body. They do not perish, though they die individually. Those who separate from this body, the enemies of unity, are those who perish. This doctrine I heard from a Chilean monk who belonged to the M.I.R. [Movimiento Izquierdista Revolucionario, Revolutionary Leftist Movement].

ALEJANDRO: "To fight to change the world is to believe in Christ."

> *God did not send his Son to the world to*
> *   condemn the world*
> *but so that the world could be saved through*
> *   him.*
> *Whoever believes in the Son of God is not*
> *   condemned;*
> *but whoever does not believe has already*
> *   been condemned*
> *for not believing in the only Son of God.*

FELIPE: "It contradicts a belief of old people, that the world, when it's past mending, is going to be destroyed in a last judgment. But here we see that there isn't any last judgment. Jesus came to mend the world and not to condemn it. Whoever is condemned, it's because that's what they want, those who don't have love (they're the ones that don't believe) and right away they're condemned by the people."

WILLIAM: "They separate from the people, they're cut off from the union of humanity which is all one, and that separation is condemnation."

> *Those who do not believe have been condemned,*
> *because when light came to the world*
> *they preferred darkness to light,*
> *because their works were evil.*
> *All those who work evil hate the light*
> *and do not approach the light*
> *so that their evil works will not be discovered.*

I: "The judgment already exists in this life, as Felipe says, and one who doesn't believe in Christ is one who doesn't love, for somewhere else, speaking of this judgment, he says: 'I was hungry and you did not feed me, I was homeless and you did not give me lodging, I was without clothing and you did not give me any.' And Jesus says here that these oppressors don't want their oppression to be discovered, they love the darkness, that is, they want the people to be kept in ignorance, and they hate the light: they don't want their exploitation to be discovered, and they make religion itself serve to cover up reality."

"I think the light is the truth, because the truth is what brings all the injustice out into the light, so the people can see it, right?"

I: "In the Gospel according to Saint John, Jesus says he is the Truth and he also says he is the Light; the truth and the light are the same thing."

WILLIAM: "Where there's light there's a gathering. Where there are people there's light: a lamp, a fire. I see the light too as a symbol of the human community, the union of humanity. And darkness is separation and solitude."

FELIPE: "So not to be in darkness is to be in a gathering."

WILLIAM: "And Jesus says that those who work evil hate the light, because anybody who's going to commit an assault, a robbery, does it in the dark. And so too people who now exploit us don't want the truth to be told in the papers or on the radio, they even forbid books, so that the country is left in the dark."

"The government has seen to it that the big strike in Managua won't be mentioned on the radio or in the newpapers. They don't want light, so they can cover up the evil they do. But the workers' action, what it's trying to do is clear things up."

I: "And maybe Jesus has gone on now to speak of light and darkness because he's speaking at night. That man has come to see him at night and surely in secret, because he was an important man, a member of the Jewish Supreme Council, and there was an antagonism between people of his class and Jesus like the one between darkness and light. Of course, in that night interview Nicodemus received the light, for afterwards he defended Jesus in the Supreme Council of the Sanhedrin."

*But those who live in accordance with the
   truth
approach the light so that it can be seen
that God is a part of what they are doing.*

"If we're in favor of a social change, we like
what's being said here."

"I see that here they're talking about practice. It says: 'What they are doing.' So they're
not just praying."

OLIVIA: "Jesus isn't talking about a God in
heaven who's far from us but a God who is love.
To see that God is a part of what they're doing
is to see love."

I: "And the God that Jesus presents is not in
heaven, as Olivia says, but in what people are
doing. If we want to look for God, that's where
we must look for him, in the liberating practice
of people."

4.

Jesus and the Samaritan Woman

(John 4:1–42)

"Give me water."
Then the Samaritan woman said to him:
"How is it that you, who are a Jew,
ask me, a Samaritan, for water?"

TOMAS: "Jesus asked for water, but it seems to me he didn't ask because he was thirsty but to be talking with the woman, because he wanted to give her a different kind of water."

LAUREANO: "There's also a lesson in the fact that he went to ask a woman of an enemy people for water. For Jesus there were no divided peoples; he belonged to all the peoples. And he teaches us not to be divided by nationalisms."

I: "He didn't care about religious differences. The reason why the Jews had no contact with the Samaritans is because they were of a different religion."

OSCAR: "Well, it seems that Jews and Samaritans didn't like each other, and she was surprised, amazed to see that an enemy was talking to her, asking her for something, and as they talked, she felt those words were getting to her heart. Then she got sincere with him, and maybe she herself didn't know what she said at that moment of truth."

Then Jesus answered her:
"If you knew the gift of God,
and who it is that is asking you for water
you would surely ask me,
and I would give you the water of life."

TOMAS: "These words are as deep as a well."

OSCAR: "It was there that she recognized it wasn't an enemy that was talking to her but that what she needed, which was love and peace, he was giving it to her."

MYRIAM, Olivia's daughter: "The gift that God gives is love."

TERESITA: "And he himself is that gift that God gives. He tells her that if she knew what God is giving, and who it is that's talking to her—It's the same thing; the one that's talking to her is love."

NATALIA: "I think maybe the water that he offers is going to take away their sins and injustices."

Jesus answered her:
"All those who drink of this water will be
*   thirsty again;*
but those who drink of the water that I give
*   will never be thirsty again.*

OLIVIA: "Surely because people who sin do it out of desire, because they're thirsty, for all desire is a thirst. And he was going to put an end to that thirst; she was going to be satisfied."

ALEJANDRO, her son: "She surely had great capacity for love and she hadn't been satisfied. She was thirsty for love, thirsty to love."

OSCAR: "I think she didn't love, because sin is not loving. She never knew about love. But, as Alejandro says, she had that thirst. She lacked love, like someone who is thirsty needs water. She didn't love; she wanted to be loved."

WILLIAM: "I think we must understand that thirst to be like the deep thirst of every human being, which is basically the thirst for love, but all other human failings too, including physical needs, are part of that thirst."

I: "Including the physical need for water, right? For we don't feel it, we who are on these islands surrounded by fresh water, but it's felt by the poor people in areas around Managua and many other places."

For the water that I shall give them
will gush forth like a spring within them
to give them eternal life.

OLIVIA: "He says the water he will give will gush forth inside of you. He gives it but it's born from us. It's God's very life that he'll give us, which is love, and that's what he calls eternal life, because it's God's life. But it's going to come out of us, it won't be stagnant, it'll be a fountain, a fountain of life."

ELVIS: "All those people who are struggling for freedom are carrying the water of life everywhere like a fountain. Freedom is like a river of life for humanity, that empties into eternal life."

Then the woman said to him:
"Lord, give me that water,
so that I won't be thirsty again,
or have to come here to this well to get water."
Jesus said to her:
"Go and call your husband,
and then come here."

TOMAS: "She was already thinking different. She was already looking for the good path. If she'd been thinking like that before, she wouldn't have asked for that water. She sees that Jesus can give her happiness."

OSCAR: "It's very nice. As a Jew he'd asked her for water. Now she, as a Samaritan, is asking him."

ROGER: "That woman had failed several times, had had several husbands, and the one she had then wasn't much. So her need was an urgent one. She was thirsty for love. For a love that would leave her satisfied."

BOSCO: "Isn't it that she's still thinking of material water and maybe has believed that he may be a kind of magician, who could spare her from carrying water, which was something very hard for her."

I: "It's possible, above all keeping in mind the magical mentality of that time. The Samaritans had a jumble of pagan religions, and they believed in many myths. . . . But even now there are many who understand the Gospel with that same magical mentality."

WILLIAM: "She was bored by all that water-carrying every day."

OLIVIA: "It's clear that what she wants is to solve that well problem, because she says it's so she won't have to go back to that well. And of course she was right. But we have to notice too that everybody was carrying that water. All she wanted to do was get rid of that problem of hers and she wasn't thinking about the others."

I: "That's a real problem that humanity has had. It's been especially the lot of women for many centuries to carry water. And that was a woman who was tired of doing it. But as Olivia says, that's a social problem. It's being solved, even though there are still very many places where it hasn't been solved. Right here in Solentiname the women or the children have to lug the water buckets home. The gift that Jesus was bringing was to solve all the problems of humanity, including the water problem. It's possible that in that place where he asked for water next to a well there's a pipe of running water, and that's a product of socialization."

OSCAR: "But what good does it do them if they're always thirsty?"

FELIPE: "With regard to Oscar's question,

what good does the water pipe do them if they're always thirsty: it seems to me that for us not to have any kind of thirst the water pipes ought to be in our consciences too."

I: "What do you say to the answer, Oscar?"

OSCAR: "It's fine by me."

I: "He says the two things have to go together, that material abundance alone isn't enough. But we can't talk about love if women still have to lug water and are enslaved in many ways, and so are men."

OLIVIA: "But it's because that love doesn't exist yet that we have slavery of women and also of men. With enough love you can have everything, even water."

OSCAR: "But it seems to me the only thing we've accomplished in many places is avoiding lugging the water bucket on your shoulder, and thirst goes right on there, which means they're not united. Or maybe they're united but they don't have enough love and nothing gets cured because thirst still exists."

IVAN: "But Jesus had offered to quench her thirst."

OSCAR: "Of course he did, as Jesus says, but not like they're talking about water pipes and drinkable water. We need something more than that."

DONALD: "But if you're in an exploited town, you have to be paying for water, every drop of water that you use to bathe in. You don't earn enough to eat and you have to pay for water, and light."

OSCAR: "That's the catch! It's a system of

exploitation. Even though you're spared the carrying of the water bucket, exploitation always exists. That's what Jesus is talking about."

I: "Oscar's right, in that place in Samaria maybe there are now water pipes but that won't mean that slavery has ended, even though that system shouldn't be called slavery but capitalism."

BOSCO: "And it's strange that when she asks him for that water, so she won't have to be carrying it, he says to her: 'Well, go and call your husband.'"

TERESITA, smiling: "It must be because he saw that the husband wasn't helping her to carry the water."

OSCAR: "No, Bosco, you have to put the bucket on your shoulder to help the woman. I imagine that what Jesus wanted is for her to tell the truth. There her thirst got a little quenched when she told the truth, when she told him that she had no husband. She told him the truth, that she had no husband. She had to be a slave, then. That thirst is killing her, and when she says this, her thirst is a little bit quenched; and she doesn't realize it."

NATALIA: "But he told her that because he knew she didn't have one, a real husband. She had often looked for love, and she was already bored with lugging that water."

OLIVIA: "Jesus knew she had a lover. He wasn't her legal husband but she had to love him, and he probably saw that even between them there wasn't much love. If there had been more love there wouldn't have been all those water trips."

OSCAR: "When she told Jesus about her intimate life she took away her thirst. When Jesus mentioned her husband she recognizes that she doesn't have one, and he says to her: You've said it well. And it's because she had no husband, because that bum she had was a lover. And maybe they didn't even love each other; they only lived together to satisfy their desire, their sin. And she wasn't going to be thirsty any more."

LAUREANO: "Jesus told her to call her husband because he wanted to give the water to them both together."

TOMAS: "I think he saw that the woman was already finding what she wanted, the pure love she'd been looking for. At that moment she felt different."

OSCAR: "Let's go on reading, Ernesto; this is very interesting."

The woman answered him:
"I have no husband."
Jesus then said to her:
"You are right to say you have no husband;
because you have had five husbands
and the one you now have is not your husband.
In this you have said the truth."

I: "Jesus makes her see that she really has had no love in her life."

LAUREANO: "Maybe she's had too much love."

I: "Too much thirst for love."

TERESITA: "She's confused about love."

I: "She was a woman divorced several times, and she was probably an unfortunate woman, oppressed by men. At that time men could reject women but women couldn't reject men. And she had seen her home destroyed several times. And it seems that the Gospel according to St. John is furnishing a symbol with this woman of Samaria. The prophets had spoken about the idolatries of that same land of Samaria as prostitution. They describe it like a wife who has forgotten her first husband, Yahweh, and who goes after her lovers, who are idols. But Isaiah had also prophesied that later Israel would no longer be called the 'Husbandless One,' and that 'the earth will have a husband.' And the Gospel in the passage before the meeting with the Samaritan woman shows us John the Baptist saying that Jesus is the Bridegroom."

> *On hearing this the woman said to him:*
> *"I see that you are a prophet.*
> *Our Samaritan ancestors worshipped God*
>   *here on this hill,*
> *but you Jews say*
> *that Jerusalem is the place where we must*
>   *adore him."*

I: "The prophets were the ones that denounced injustices, which were the idolatry or prostitution of Israel. And now it seems that this is no longer a woman with a problem of her private life. The Samaritan woman is Samaria that has recognized in Jesus the voice of the prophets."

OSCAR: "There she's realizing that it's not a question of a water pipe that they were going to put in their houses to avoid carrying water. Man, that water fountain is beginning to show. What Jesus meant, I figure, is that you have to give yourself to other people with love: sacrificing yourself to put an end to slavery and exploitation; and we can do a lot through the people. That's what Jesus meant, he wanted to tell the Samaritan woman to give herself, not to go around with falseness, and to love. Many people in this country have died for this cause. What Jesus was coming to do was to bring us out of slavery."

I: "The main antagonism between the Jews and the Samaritans was about the temple. The Jews were saying it was necessary to adore God in the Temple of Jerusalem, and the Samaritans that it was on their hill where there was a temple that rivalled that of Jerusalem and that was very close to the place where Jesus was talking with the Samaritan woman. She's asking him which of the two religions is the true one."

Jesus answered her: "Believe me, woman, the hour is coming when you will adore the Father

*without having to come to this hill
or go to Jerusalem."*

TOMAS: "He wants to tell her that God is everywhere, not just in Jerusalem and on that hill, and that you can adore him anywhere."

LAUREANO: "I think there's no need to have divisions among people. When everybody's united and loves each other, God will be there with them and they won't have to go anywhere to adore him."

"Not even to the churches?" somebody asks him. And he answers: "People gather in the churches."

I: "The first Christians had no temples. 'Church' in Greek is a secular word that means 'meeting.' I have read that in the Old Testament also the Bible uses scarcely any religious words, only lay words that were later given a religious sense. For example, the word 'cult' came from a military term and was equivalent to our word 'militance.' And in the New Testament, when religious words are used, it's to give them back a secular sense, as when Saint Paul says that the temple is people."

MANUEL: "That's why we don't think it's bad to smoke in church, and we're smoking while we're making these commentaries, because this place isn't sacred. What's sacred for us is the unity we have here."

FELIPE: "Men, women, children, old people, those are the sacred temples of God, and these are the temples that are respected in Cuba."

OLIVIA: "But here in Nicaragua that time

that some groups of young Christians seized the lecterns to demand freedom for political prisoners, there were people that said they were profaning the temple."

I: "One of the accusations made against Jesus when they condemned him to death was that he had said he was going to destroy the temple. The evangelists say that was slander and that they couldn't prove it; but that accusation may have had some basis, and they deny it because they were very insistent on defending Jesus. At least it's clear that he was against the temple; he not only had called it a thieves' cave but he'd said not one stone would be left upon another. He'd also said that God was already abandoning the temple. And to the Samaritan woman here he was announcing its immediate disappearance. To say this and to say that he would cause the destruction is almost the same. The Jews' slander would be to say he was planning to do it with terrorist methods."

FELIPE: "The Jews, like the Samaritans, were very alienated through religion. Jesus tells the woman that's going to end, that God's going to be worshipped everywhere where others are loved."

I: "Christ says that neither of the two religions are going to be needed, but he doesn't talk of a new religion."

OSCAR: "Well, it seems to me that Christ wanted to show the woman that it's not worthwhile to worry about religion, that God's not interested in the temple, in people going to worship him at a fixed place, like a hill or the church of Jerusalem. It seems it doesn't matter to him. We're here in this church and he doesn't care about the church, as a building. What he cares about is for all of us to love him. Now that's really to be knowing what love is, what God is. It seems they only loved themselves, you see? And Christ there was showing them that to love God they had to love others, all the people, or really the whole world."

MANUEL: "But right after that we see he makes a distinction between the Samaritans and the Jews:

> *"You Samaritans do not know what you worship:*
> *but we know what we worship;*
> *for freedom comes from the Jews."*

FELIPE: "I think the world has always had a lot of doctrines; some go one way and some the other, and it's the same thing nowadays. But there's only one that carries the people forward, toward freedom. And Jesus must have been conscious that in the Jews there was really a true doctrine of freedom, of complete freedom, in the writings they had. And that's the difference he sees with the other religions."

ALEJANDRO: "Of course, freedom as an idea comes from the Jewish religion. But he just says it comes from there. It comes in order to spread everywhere. Freedom is for everybody, people of all the religions and people without religion, too."

I: "The whole Bible is a constant denunciation of injustice and a constant defense of poor people, widows, orphans; and it is constantly setting up the goal of humanity, a perfect society. That's the difference between the Bible and all the pagan religions, which considered the world as finished, unable to change, and they were on the side of the status quo, oppression. (And the Samaritans had a mixture of various pagan religions.) What Marx says, that God always appears on the side of the dominant power, is very true of the god of most religions, but not of the God of the Bible. Although in practice, when the Jews were unfaithful to the God of the Bible, they also had an alienating religion, allied with power. And that's what Christ came to fight against."

OSCAR: "Ernesto, this question is bothering me. It was from the Jews that freedom came, says Christ. But why did freedom come from there? If freedom came from there, why did they screw him? The Jews knew the true God, who was justice; the Samaritans didn't know the God they worshiped and they had no idea of who he was, but in spite of worshiping a god in ignorance, they weren't sure of who they were worshiping. Christ went to a woman who's a Samaritan, and it seems he knew they were going to welcome him there with love."

I: "The Gospel said at the beginning of this passage that the Pharisees were alarmed be-

cause Jesus was getting more popular than
John the Baptist, and Jesus left Judea. It's
clear that he is fleeing. He had seen the fate of
John the Baptist. And then he passes through
Samaria. He tells the Samaritan woman that
freedom comes from the Jews, but it's a freedom that he's fleeing from."

But the hour is coming, and it is here,
when those who really worship the Father
will worship him in spirit and in truth.

TOMAS: "Wherever there is the spirit of love,
he's being really worshiped."

FELIPE: "That means they're not going to
worship him just by word. Because many of us
used to pray (and there are still a lot of people
who pray that way), but it was to a God who
lived who knows where. Jesus teaches that we
have to love God, but in our neighbors; the one
that loves his neighbors loves God."

I: "Jesus says the hour is going to come and it
has already come. That seems to be a contradiction. In another passage, speaking
about his message resurrecting the dead, he
says that hour will come and it has already
come. The kingdom is to come and it has already come. One of the liberation theologians,
Father Juan Luis Segundo, says that the
Bible doesn't understand the world as an un-
changeable reality but as a process in evolution, but at that time in which the concept of
evolution did not exist and there were no
words to express it, the Bible has to face those

contradictions: something that already exists and doesn't yet exist."

God is Spirit,
and those who worship him
must do so in spirit and in truth.

I: " 'God is Spirit' doesn't mean that he is immaterial. 'Spirit' to the Jews meant breath of life. The opposite of 'spirit' is not 'matter' but 'death.' God is life, and he is the one who instills life in us. His life, or spirit, which he instills in us, is love. It's the same as saying that it's the love that there is among us."

"Many rich people can worship God in the sanctuary, but they're exploiting, they're screwing humanity; then that's not true, it's a lie, a hypocrisy. They don't really worship. But there are others who don't even go into church to hear Mass. It's true of many young men who don't even mention God, and yet they go off to fight a battle to defend the oppressed, and those people, it seems to me, they do really and truly worship."

The woman said to him:
"I know that the Messiah is going to come;
and when he comes he will explain every-
thing to us."

FRANCISCO: "She was a little mixed up, maybe."

ROGER: "I don't think she was mixed up. She

was a woman who needed love and she was expecting that some time a messiah was going to come who was going to solve all the problems."

> *Jesus said to her:*
> *"I am that one,*
> *the one who is talking to you."*

FELIPE: "She may always have been a little confused, because she couldn't find which religion was the truth. She was hoping somebody would come and explain it to her, but when Jesus tells her that God is now going to be worshiped without religion, she doesn't understand that. She says that when the Messiah comes, the Liberator, he'll explain everything to us; and he has to tell her: the one who is explaining this to you is already the Liberator."

I: "Among the Jews Jesus never said he was the Messiah, and he forbade anyone to say it. It's clear that it was to avoid repression, for he told it clearly to that Samaritan woman and she went and told all the people."

FRANCISCO: "She never imagined that the Messiah was going to come to where she was in the shape of an enemy that went up to her to ask for water."

OSCAR: "And she was really startled. But the truth is that Jesus approaches all of us who like her have been evil, that is, all of us who are thirsty for love."

We later saw that the disciples came with food, but Jesus wouldn't eat, and he said to them:

My food is to do the will of him who sent me, and to fulfill his work.

FELIPE: "He was very interested in the work he was doing, with that woman who had gone to inform all the people, and that's why he had no appetite. His hunger is to do the will of God. That happens with real leaders, who often forget to eat or sleep because of what they're doing."

I: "He says that his food is to do the work of God in the kingdom. And that is also the work that God has begun since he created the world, and that Jesus is going to fulfill."

FRANCISCO: "But Jesus is going to fulfill the work through us; he's not going to do it all by himself. And the work hasn't ended."

ALEJANDRO: "For each of us that work will be ended only when we die."

FRANCISCO: "Well, when life ends, then you stop working. But some will be freed, maybe those that you freed, the way Christ did with many. Many were conscientized to carry that conscientization across the centuries. When each of us dies, there our work ends, but others begin, and so that's the way the work has reached us."

I: "The same reflection that you have made is the one that Jesus makes next, looking at the fields that were recently sown:

You say: "It's four months until harvest";
but I say to you: Raise your eyes and see the
* yellow fields ready for reaping.*
And the reaper is paid,
and he reaps a harvest for life eternal;
and the sower shares in the joy of the reaper.
The saying is true:
"One sows and it is someone else who reaps."
I have sent you to harvest where others have
* worked.*

LAUREANO: "All the work that's done on earth is a continuation of the work that God began. With their work the workers are fulfilling the world, or rather they continue creating the world. In society there shouldn't be anybody who doesn't work. Anyone who doesn't work doesn't eat. Right now there's one part, the biggest part, that works for everybody, and the part that consumes most is the one that doesn't work. But work wouldn't be finished in the perfect society; the machines wouldn't run by themselves or be manufactured by themselves."

OSCAR: "What Christ comes to say, do you know what it is? That we're finally going to work the good earth that's going to give us a good harvest, while up to now we've been sowing on stones or on uncleared land and therefore the work gives us nothing. Others are working the good earth, like Cuba, where there aren't any more prejudices or divisions, and they're working like brothers and sisters; there's love among everybody and there's love for all peoples. I'm afraid I can't explain it."

I: "Jesus says that his hunger, his burning desire, is to fulfill the work of his Father, but Laureano is right: that doesn't mean we're going to stop working. When they criticized Jesus for curing a paralytic on a day of rest, he answered: 'My Father always works and I also work.' The Jews kept the Sabbath in memory of the day when God rested after the six days of creation. But according to Jesus, God has always continued with his creative work, and now he comes to help in that work, to complete the creation. And as Francisco has said: together with us."

IVAN (one of the youngest): "Does that mean that in perfect communism there's going to be no Sabbath; every day's going to be a working day?"

I: "Well, work is going to be like rest and rest will be like work. There won't be the distinction there is now between rest and work. It'll be like when you go fishing, you have fun fishing and at the same time you're doing some work."

OSCAR: "I believe the rest that God took after the creation, you know what it is? It's humankind. And our rest is the same, it's getting together. Like we are today, which is a day of rest, but it's so that we can all get together, so we can feel happy. But the body always works, right? Rest is being happy; it's looking at each other's faces and greeting each other and if possible, well, having a drink. Well, that's a rest for me, I don't know about you. Look, when I go to have a drink with another guy I feel happy. When I'm working I'm talking, but I'm working; and it's different to be at rest for an hour, and to see their faces, and to be talking, like we are now. We spend six long days of the week all split up, not seeing our friends; here we're seeing each other and greeting each other: how you doing? This is a rest that God created, to be together here. But God isn't resting, he's always giving us his spirit, pouring it out so there'll be this love among us."

OLIVIA: "I think that rest isn't simply this Sunday rest but the rest that comes from a change, because with a change we rested from the oppression we had. It isn't rest from work: because there'll be more work."

FRANCISCO: "They used to say that in socialist countries like Cuba they're sowing on good ground. I think they're also harvesting now. Now they're trying to carry the grain somewhere else. There many people spilled their blood so they could be at ease. Now nobody's hungry."

WILLIAM: "Rest is going to be when we all enjoy the abundance of the work of everybody. And work is going to be very joyful."

FELIPE: "But now if you lie down to sleep and you know you don't have anything to eat, you can't rest."

OSCAR: "That's what I want to make clear, that we've all got to get together and not be damned fools. Together we're going to make the truth win, what Jesus went to teach to those gypsies—what's the word?—Samaritans. And let's not be afraid of death; death is a passageway to life."

LAUREANO: *"That* kind of death."

5.

The Bread of Life

(John 6:25–29)

We read the words that, according to Saint John, Jesus said in a synagogue to the people who were following him after the multiplication of the loaves. Before beginning to comment on the first verses, JULIO GUEVARA, JUNIOR, said: "This Gospel seems real crazy. All it talks about is the bread of life and salvation and heaven and eternal life."

I tell you the truth,
you seek me out because you stuffed your-
*   selves,*
and not because you have understood the
*   miraculous signs.*
Do not work for the food that will come to an
*   end*
but for the food that endures and gives you
*   eternal life.*

ALEJANDRO: "We see clearly that those signs, feeding or curing, were to make us see how society should be organized. He wanted them to learn to perform miracles also, working all together, without exploiting each other, so there would be bread, health, and all the rest."

OSCAR: "I think the true food he was bringing was union among all people—love. He wasn't coming just to multiply the rice and the kidney beans."

OLIVIA: "The bread that's used up is the bread that's sought selfishly, and the bread that gives life is the bread we seek as a community. That bread produces eternal life because it produces the kingdom."

"I want to add here something like what Doña Olivia says: and it's that for Jesus the true life is a life without injustice, and that's the life of that bread, the community of people, which he brings. But what the system of injustice and exploitation produces is death."

I: "They hadn't understood the sign or signal of the distribution of the bread: they hadn't understood that symbol."

> *This is the food that the Son of Man will give*
> *you,*
> *because God the Father has put on him his*
> *seal.*

"Us *campesinos* and illiterates always let ourselves be deceived by people who offer us a mouthful of food or anything that we'll use up quickly, even though afterwards we'll be worse off than before. And we don't let ourselves be persuaded by people that offer us a lesson to lead more of a community life, which would be the true life."

I: "That bread that doesn't last is like the distribution of grain that Somoza has just made up north, to win over the *campesinos*, with which he's not going to get anybody out of misery. On the other hand, Jesus is telling them that the miraculous food they've had hasn't solved any of their problems, that what it's all about is to change the world, to replace the system of injustice with a system of love. And that's the bread he has brought, his word, because he's the message of love that God has sent us, and that's why he says God has placed on him 'his seal,' as on a letter."

DOÑA NATALIA: "There are so many workers that are just hanging on. All that work. Earning pennies. Working exhausted there, tired out, the poor man, and they make him do all that work, and he always gives in, puts up with that. His food, rice and beans, may not be well cooked. If he doesn't work he doesn't earn. It's tough, it's tough. And Christ is saying they shouldn't put up with it."

WILLIAM: "Jesus probably had in mind all those workers who've been hanging on as Doña Natalia says, all through history. And he tells them they mustn't work for the bread that doesn't last, any more than for better salaries, as the developmentalists want. The world has to be changed. His hearers understand that he's proposing a change, when they ask him what plan he's bringing them."

Then they asked him:
"What must we do to bring about the things
that God wants us to do?"
And Jesus answered them:
"What God wants you to do
is to believe in the one he has sent."

ESPERANZA, Olivia's daughter: "He means that anybody that comes along talking like he talks is also sent by God."

FELIPE: "He was coming to teach that everybody ought to get together and love each other. And that's why he tells them to believe in him. If they believed in him injustice would end and the world would change."

MANUEL: "It's that, if they believed in him, they had to believe in the whole message that he was bringing. They had first to believe in his person in order to believe in his word and to carry out his word."

OSCAR: "And believing in him meant believing that God had sent him, that he wasn't just shooting a line about himself, that the revolution he was bringing was the will of God."

I: "They have asked him what they should do to carry out God's plan. He doesn't answer that; he tells them that God's plan is that they believe that God sent him. He means that they must believe that he has been sent as a messiah, as a liberator, and that is also the same as believing in liberation. The listeners have understood that, and they remember the first liberation from Egyptian slavery. They tell him that Moses showed signs of being a

liberator sent by God, as when he fed them
'bread from heaven,' and they ask Jesus what
signs he can show."

> *Jesus answered them: "I tell you the truth:*
> *It was not Moses who gave you bread from*
>   *heaven;*
> *my Father is the one who gives you the true*
>   *bread from heaven,*
> *because the bread that God gives*
> *is the bread that has come down from heaven*
> *and that gives life to men."*

"As Oscar wisely said, that bread that he
talks about is love, and he has come to bring
love here to the earth through his message, to
make us give up self-interest and seek union
and communism. That message is a loaf of
bread brought down from heaven to nourish
us."

OSCAR: "If all we worry about is crops and
business, maybe we become more selfish and
more divided. But love unites us, and that's
what we must concentrate on, always love,
union, companionship, not letting the others
perish. Many times the more you have the
more you want to have and you forget about
the others; that abundance, then, doesn't give
us true life; it may be that there's a lot of crops
and injustice continues. They ate that manna
in the desert, but it didn't change them or
straighten them out."

I: "Scripture said, as the Jews have quoted it
here, that the manna was a 'loaf from heaven,'

but Jesus tells them the revolutionary thing that it's not true that that loaf was from heaven. It has now been discovered that that manna was really a sweet, white syrup that drips from the tree called tamarind, and which the desert bedouins still eat in that region. And Jesus says: there isn't any bread like that come down from heaven. The only bread that comes from heaven is the word of love, which he is transmitting, and which will give humanity a new life."

> *I am the bread that gives life.*
> *He who comes to me will never be hungry;*
> *and he who believes in me will never be*
>   *thirsty.*

OLIVIA: "If there's love, there's no hunger. That hunger for exploitation and thirst to get more. Those ambitions are hunger and thirst, desires never satisfied. They always want to own more. But if you have love, then you're full, you're satisfied, you're happy."

"Here in Nicaragua there's a lot of propaganda against Fidel Castro, and they say there are shortages there. What they don't think about is that whatever there is is for everybody. And the truth is that everybody's satisfied there, because nobody's in need and nobody has too much; everybody has the same. But here, no matter how rich they are, they are never satisfied; they always want more. There, in a place where there's justice, they don't have the thirst that we have here."

I: "Not long ago I was reading a scientist who says it has been discovered that the greatest human need, the one all other needs come from, is for sociability, for cooperation; in other words, the greatest hunger and thirst of people is the hunger and thirst for love. And that's the thirst that Jesus says he has come to quench."

WILLIAM: "And this has a lot to do with that other thing that he said, about the hunger and thirst for justice that would be satisfied."

> *Everything that the Father gives me*
> *comes to me,*
> *and those who come to me*
> *I shall not throw out.*

LAUREANO: "The poor, the helpless, those are the ones that the Father gave to him."

GLORIA: "They wouldn't be the middle-class ones, because they had no confidence in him."

ELVIS: "And it seems to me that all people struggling for justice anywhere in the world have come to Christ, even when they don't call him Christ and they don't call themselves Christians. And he doesn't throw them out. Many Christians believe that atheist revolutionaries aren't with Christ. But he says he doesn't throw them out, if they're seeking communion with other people, which means seeking him."

NATALIA, Elvis's mother: "Anybody that receives the teaching of Christ goes where he goes and seeks union with others, and if you're united you can't be reseparated."

FELIPE: "This seems very interesting, because there are many who know their Bible well, but they're far away from love. It's one thing to know the Scriptures and it's quite a different thing to put them into practice. A Che, a Fidel, have put them into practice."

> *And the will of him who sent me*
> *is that I not lose any of those that he has*
>   *given me*
> *but that I resurrect them on the final day.*
> *The will of my Father is that all those*
> *who look at the Son and believe in him have*
>   *eternal life.*

OLIVIA: "Here he makes a promise with us, with those of us who accept his message, and it's very important, what he promises, to resurrect us all on the last day, the day of total liberation. And there wouldn't be total liberation if there wasn't also resurrection."

ALEJANDRO: "Love makes a promise to anyone that surrenders to him. Love then takes charge of you and manages you."

I: "Jesus has said that we cannot be lost, the will of the Father is for nobody to be lost, and we'd be lost if we were to disappear with death."

> *At this point the Jews began to criticize*
>   *Jesus,*

because he said:
"I am the bread that came down from
    heaven."
And they said: "Isn't this Jesus, the son of
    Joseph?
We know his father and mother.
How does he say he came down from
    heaven?"

FELIPE: "It's obvious they didn't believe in him, and they didn't believe because they were expecting some kind of liberation to come from heaven, like something magical."

GLORIA: "And above all they didn't believe in him because he was the son of a workman. They kept rubbing it in that he was the son of a carpenter. If he'd been rich and powerful maybe it would have been easier for them to think he'd come down from heaven."

BOSCO: "Their reaction was from the idea they had of heaven, and that God is in a place where you can't reach him, but Jesus is telling them that the descent from heaven was that God came up out of the working class."

WILLIAM: "And the same way now, many religious Christians are waiting for a liberation falling down from heaven and not a liberation that rises up from the people."

BOSCO: "And imperialism encourages that religiosity so the people will keep passive facing injustices, waiting only for that salvation from above: it's enough to hear those Protestant radio programs that talk only about heaven to realize that."

Jesus said to them:
"Stop criticizing.
None can come to me if they are not brought
*   by the Father that sent me;*
and I shall resurrect them on the last day.
In the books of the prophets it is said:
'God will teach them all.'
So all those who listen to the Father and
*   learn from him come to me."*

EDUARDO: "That's very strange."

GERARDO: "In the Bible God was teaching his revolutionary message to very few, practically only to the prophets. Now with the present revolutions the whole people thinks and talks like the prophets. In a country that's making its revolution, there are thousands, millions of prophets. They've been taught by the Father, although they don't know it, and they identify with Jesus."

ELVIS: "That Father who sent Jesus, who made him rise up from the people, is the same one who sends us toward Jesus, who joins us with him, and makes Jesus and the people into a single thing."

MYRIAM: "I believe all who struggle for liberation, in any part of the world, are also sent by the Father like Jesus."

LAUREANO: "They are generally persecuted and killed, but according to the words of Jesus it doesn't matter if they persecute you and kill you because on the last day you're going to be alive."

It is not that someone has seen the Father;
the only one who has seen him is the one who
has come from God.
I tell you the truth:
They who believe in me
have eternal life.

MANUEL: "To know God we must know Jesus, who is humanity."

OSCAR: "We haven't seen him, but we've heard the word of Jesus Christ, who is the one who has seen him and has told us how he is: he's love."

OLIVIA: "This seems to me very important, especially for us poor people who are always waiting for a salvation that will come from heaven; we settle for praying to God, and Jesus is saying: who's seen him?"

FELIPE: "It seems he wanted to tell those Jews all their practices were inventions."

I: "He doesn't deny that God exists, but he says you can't see him."

OLIVIA: "And you can't love him either because you can't see him. And because of that we also have this: how are we going to love God, who we can't see, if we don't love our neighbors, who we *can* see."

I: "We can't see him but we *can* love each other and that is to know God according to Saint John. It is to possess him, as you can possess a lover."

FELIPE: "I think he wants us to put aside all false information that we've been having about God and that has removed us from the true God, who is love."

WILLIAM: "It's interesting that he doesn't say that anyone who believes in him *will* have eternal life, but that he *has* eternal life. So we see that eternal life is something we already have in this life."

BOSCO: "Christ was living in the perfect society of God; just as Che left his ministry in Cuba to carry the revolution somewhere else, Christ left that heavenly society to come to preach heaven here on earth."

I: "So that humanity can be one just as he and the Father are one, so that humanity can be like the Trinity, and have heaven be made here on earth, isn't that it?"

I am the bread that gives life
that came down from heaven;
those who eat this bread will live forever.
The bread that I shall give is my own body.
I shall give it for the life of the world.

OSCAR: "His body he gave up so there'd be justice in the world; that's why he says that it's to give life, and that's why he calls it 'bread.'"

GERARDO: "They killed that body but it goes on living, giving life to the world, and all who live for others are also part of that body, are bread that gives life to the world."

"And the Eucharist?"

I: "Christ chose the image of a community supper to represent the union of people, who should share all goods in common. In the New Testament the same Greek word *koinonia* (which is like saying 'communism') designates the Eucharist, the community of wealth, and the union that exists between people and God. When we share the bread of the Eucharist, we share in the body of Christ and we unite with the whole people, with whom he is identified, and with God who is a single thing with him. But the Eucharist is only a figure to mean the real union of people in the whole society."

LAUREANO: " It seems to me that if we were all well organized in a socialist society, or even better, communist, we'd all be sharing the bread and everything else, as we do in the Eucharist. It wouldn't any longer be the Eucharist that we have at Mass but we would celebrate it every day eating in perfect brotherhood and sharing in all the wealth all alike: it would be a Super Eucharist."

> *I tell you the truth,*
> *if you don't eat the body of the Son of Man*
> *   and drink his blood,*
> *you have no life.*
> *He who eats my body and drinks my blood*
> *   has life eternal;*
> *and I shall resurrect him on the last day.*

LAUREANO: "It could be that eating his body and drinking his blood would mean that we could be like him, could share his life, and that we'd sacrifice our lives for the lives of others."

NATALIA: " 'And I shall resurrect him on the

last day.' He's repeating it a lot, but Christ never talked nonsense. He's repeating it so we'll believe it."

FELIPE: "It seems to me that love is eternal and that it never ends and if you live in love then what you do never ends either. Love has to win out over evil, and therefore love has to lead an eternal life, but evil won't be eternal; it's going to end."

I: "Jesus talks a lot about resurrection, which in the language of the Bible is the same as saying 'wake up.' But he doesn't give us the slightest indication of how it's going to be, so it's useless for us to try to imagine it. In another passage from the Gospel according to Saint John, Jesus says the resurrection has already begun."

> *He who eats my body and drinks my blood*
> *lives in union with me, and I with him.*
> *The Father who sent me has life,*
> *and I live through him;*
> *in the same way,*
> *he who feeds on me will live through me.*

I: "He is united with God and shares the life of God, and if we are united with him, which means to be united with others, we form part of his body and we share in his life, which is the life of God. And that life is the resurrection, of Christ and of us, of the whole body."

JULIO RAMON: "He repeats the same thing a lot." [And with his finger to his temple he gives the signal that Jesus is crazy].

BONICHE: "He repeats a lot, but each repetition is a little different."

ALEJANDRO: "And that repetition sounds very poetical."

NATALIA (emphatically): "And it's so we'll believe it."

6.

The Adulterous Woman

(John 8:1–11)

"Master, this woman has been taken in adul-
   tery.
The law of Moses orders us to stone this kind
   of woman.
What do you say?"
They said this to lay a trap for him
and so to have an excuse to accuse him.

FELIPE: "Those are the same ones that are
now opposed to the Gospel, the ones that oppress the people. And now like then they appear as defenders of the law."

WILLIAM: "If he said, 'Let them kill her,'
they would ask how someone who preached
love could condemn a poor woman to be stoned
to death. And if he said, 'Let them not kill her,'
he was also screwed because they'd say: 'Aha!
This man is contradicting the law of Moses.' "

ALEJANDRO: "But Jesus got out of it very
well. They thought he had to answer one thing
or the other: he either approved of the law,

which was unjust, or he approved of adultery.
We too sometimes are asked difficult questions, for example, about violence: it seems we
can answer them only one way or the other;
but we manage to find a third answer, like
Jesus did, which is the wiser answer."

MANUEL: "And here we see the cruelty of
these defenders of the law. They didn't care
what the woman had done; they were taking
her to Jesus for him to condemn her, taking
advantage of a woman's weakness to screw
Jesus. It's the same now in our system; they'll
use anything to attack people who want justice."

> *Then Jesus bent down and began to write on*
> *the ground with his finger.*

"Maybe it was to show them he didn't think
they were important."

"Would he be drawing a little landscape?"

"He could have been writing a message,
something about love. But they didn't even
read that; they were just interested in pla-
guing him."

> *But as they went on questioning him,*
> *he stood up and said to them:*
> *"The one of you who is without sin,*
> *let him cast the first stone."*
> *And he bent down again and went on writing*
> *on the ground.*

OLIVIA: "Jesus observed that, although the

woman was an adulteress, there were others who had committed much greater sins, and they were the ones who were oppressing the people, and nobody was killing them. There's a lot of harsh criticism nowadays of the actions of a woman like that, and they don't even see or denounce all the oppression and all the injustice there is. That's why, when they bring Jesus one of those women, who was probably a single woman, not one of the great ladies, his response is very clever."

WILLIAM: "We have to take into account too that Jesus was in favor of equality of men and women; this is very important now, when there's so much talk of women's liberation. Later Saint Paul would say that with Christ there are no longer Jews and Greeks, masters and slaves, men and women. And Christ could have been writing down the adulteries of those who were accusing that woman. Because if that was the punishment for that woman, why shouldn't they stone to death the men who do the same?"

TERESITA: "I believe all the men who were accusing that woman were adulterers."

OSCAR: "It seems there were great oppressions at that time, right? And one of them was that a woman was treated like dirt, because if she, the female, did it, it was terrible; if the man did it they didn't even notice."

OLIVIA: "It was the *machismo* of that time, which was very strong, but we go right on having it in our time. That woman didn't commit adultery all by herself, and the man she committed adultery with, they didn't accuse him."

OSCAR: "Yes, they didn't bring him."

I: "In the Gospels called the Apocrypha, which are fictitious but which may have some authentic details preserved by tradition, there is a mysterious saying of Jesus, which in the light of what you have said becomes very clear, and it sounds as if he had really said it (nobody else would dare to invent it): Jesus' phrase is that in the kingdom of heaven 'men will be like women, and women like men.' "

ROGER PEREZ, the young painter from Managua: "The case of this woman is important for us in Latin America. We need to learn this lesson of tolerance and pardon and love in the case of the adultery of the woman. We've had a tradition opposed to this for centuries, the *machismo* tradition. Among us the adulterous woman is still condemned to death, and not just in songs. There are phrases that we all repeat: 'If she did anything like that to me, I'd kill her, that bitch.' This isn't Christian, it isn't revolutionary."

WILLIAM: "Adultery is a minor sin, man, compared with others. If a woman goes with a man, well, it's a sin. I don't say it isn't, especially if harm is done to the man or woman comrade or the children are going to suffer or there are other consequences. But compared with the harm that comes from other sins, it's not one of the most serious ones."

I: "It's more serious to stone the woman to death, right?"

On hearing this,
they went away one by one,
beginning with the oldest.

OLIVIA: "Because the oldest were the most sinful, the most adulterous maybe. Or robbers, exploiters."

WILLIAM: "And they were the ones too with the most prestige, the most venerable, and the bosses. At that time society was run by the oldest, never by a young man. And those were the worst ones too, corrupted by power."

"The oldest ones are always the most evil."

ROGER PEREZ: "Like certain very corrupt, very perverse, very criminal old men that we have in the government: Lorenzo Guerrero, Luis Manuel Debayle."

OSCAR: "From what Christ said it's clear that those bastards were evil old men."

I: "And let's not forget that they were religious people: the Bible stresses at the beginning that they were 'teachers of the law and Pharisees.' They have come talking to him about Moses. But Jesus accuses those religious people and puts himself on the side of an adulteress."

OSCAR: "What a relief at that moment for that woman, right? Because even though the public had known all about her, there they saw that the others were doing the same things, although they were doing them secretly. She was surprised, it seems to me, that her sins were minor and that the others came out worse than she did; they were no better, and now they had no heart to attack her."

WILLIAM: "They come with this woman to Jesus invoking the law of Moses; the law has always been used to oppress the people. And Jesus' answer invalidates not only this particular law that they're asking him about, but the whole judicial system."

OSCAR: "Man, this Moses made that law tough! To stone a woman who had committed a fault! To throw hundreds of rocks at her that could kill her! It would have been more humane to kill her with a *machete* blow, or with a pistol. Others committed other worse things and it wasn't known except among themselves. If they treated the faults of everybody with this same severity, they'd all have put an end to each other."

I: "That law that they were invoking was an ancient law, from the time when society was very barbaric."

OSCAR: "Yes, but who made the mistake of making that law?"

WILLIAM: "It was no error, man; those laws were less savage than others they'd had before."

MANUEL: "But weren't those laws inspired in Moses by God?"

WILLIAM: "But Jesus makes it clear that what was progress earlier can later be a step backward. They face Jesus with tradition, and Jesus shows them that to maintain tradition is equal to maintaining injustice."

I: "The law of the universe is the law of evolution, that's the supreme law of God. Any other law that tries to hold onto the past is an unjust law. Father Juan Luis Segundo says that in the language of the New Testament 'sin' is equal to conservatism: it's the attitude opposed to change."

JULIO: "Jesus is talking there just about the case of one woman, but I think we ought now to relate it to everything. Not just to women but to everybody, men and women, to everybody that's being killed, if not with stones or machetes or pistols, then with hunger and all the other tortures of exploitation. That case of the women who were being persecuted by the law is the same as all poor people who've been crushed by the rich."

GLORIA: "And women? They're more oppressed because they're women. That's why, to make us see that the law is unjust and oppressive, Jesus gave the example of that woman who, according to the law, was to be stoned."

> *"Woman, where are those who were accusing you?*
> *Did none condemn you?"*
> *She said: "No, Lord, none."*
> *Then Jesus said to her:*
> *"Nor will I condemn you;*
> *go and sin no more."*

MANUEL: "And I bet she didn't sin again. She was freed from the law and also from the sin."

ELVIS: "We were dealing with that same

thing yesterday in the meeting of the youth group, what to do when a comrade is at fault, and we said we ought to give him advice, persuade him to reform himself."

MYRIAM: "Jesus teaches us how to change our lives. If we've sinned, not to go on sinning."

ALEJANDRO, her brother: "I don't believe he said only one sentence. It's possible he said many things to her, he was with her quite a while, and he left her all straightened out."

MYRIAM (who said earlier that Jesus maybe wrote some message): "And she *would* read what he wrote on the ground."

7.

"I Am the Light of the World"

(John 8:12–20)

We were at the meeting hut and we had lunched on some sawfish brought by the Madrigales, from La Venada Island.

I am the light of the world;
those who follow me will have the light that
*   gives them life*
and they will never walk in darkness.

OLIVIA: "In the dark nobody can see and we stumble when we walk. But with light we can go very well along the road."

ELVIS: "He's the light of the oppressed people. He lights the road of liberation for us, and that's why he says he's the light that gives us life."

"He brought unity and love to the world and that's the light of the world. And it's what gives us life too. And anybody that follows that light won't be walking in darkness."

"Ernesto, I think the darkness Jesus is talk-

ing about is the alienation into which the
people have sunk. The people have been kept
in the dark by the powerful, and they haven't
even realized they were oppressed. Even religion has been used to keep them down, and
when the people begin to realize it, it's because they receive the light of Jesus."

"Humanity's starting to see that light; it's
the revolution that's rising up all over the
world."

"And darkness and light are opposite
things that can't unite. The light is teaching
us to live a really human life. But the darkness of the rich produces death: death in the
proletariat, through murder or through
hunger, or infant mortality, or lack of
medicines; and death among themselves too,
for some of them are victims of others."

I added that in the Gospel of Saint John
Jesus says: "I am the light; I am the truth; I
am the road; I am the life." All that's the
same as saying: "I am the revolution." He
stresses above all that he is the light, and we
can say that the universe originated from
light. The stars are concentrations of light
and heat. The life of the earth proceeds from
the light and heat of one star, the sun. The
increasing socialization of humankind, love,
is a new phase of the same process that began
with the concentration of the stars. When
Jesus says he is the light, it seems to me he's
also saying: "I am the evolution."

"I think we've already found enough light
in this verse."

> *I know where I came from and where I am*
>   *going;*
> *but you do not know where I come from*
> *or where I am going.*

MANUEL: "Well, he comes from God, who's love. The three persons are united in a single God through love; he comes from love and he goes toward love, to establish love among humankind, the union of all humankind by means of love. Those people didn't know that."

ALEJO: "They thought they knew those things they had written down, and those bastards didn't know shit, because they had a backward mentality. Like guys you meet now, that don't even have an idea of what a revolutionary action is; they don't know where history's going or where it comes from."

WILLIAM: "Those gentlemen didn't know where the little carpenter had come from, or where he was going to get with that doctrine. And it seems to me that even now there are lots who call themselves Christians and they don't know which way that doctrine of Christ is going, where the changes in the world are going. And they don't know where those changes come from. They don't know that the impulse for social revolutions comes from God."

ALEJANDRO: "I remember what Fidel said in his speech: 'History will absolve me.' *He* knew where history was going."

BOSCO: "I don't think even the great leaders know anything about how far love is going to

go, nobody; and I dare to state that nobody
has known, only Christ; nobody else can know
what there'll be after the objectives we're
now seeing."

ɪ: "Marx used to say that he didn't know
what would come after communism. Christ
declares that he is the evolution (or the revolution, which is the same thing) and that he
knows where he comes from and where he's
going."

> *You judge according to the world.*
> *I do not judge anybody,*
> *and if I judge my judgment is sound,*
> *for I do not judge by myself,*
> *the Father that sent me judges along with*
>   *me.*
> *In your law it is written*
> *that when two witnesses say the same thing,*
> *we must believe them;*
> *well, then, I myself am a witness in my favor,*
> *and the Father who has sent me is the other*
>   *witness.*

"His judgment is based on reality, based on
justice. Not like they judge in the courts in this
unjust system: only the poor get sentenced,
not the rich."

"He's telling them they judge according to
the unjust laws they have, as we might say
now: the laws of the state that we have. They
judge according to the laws of injustice, because their system is unjust, and that's why
they judged him and sentenced him to death."

OSCAR: "He's telling them that when two witnesses speak, they're believed; but maybe those witnesses say lies to ruin you; two false witnesses can sentence a Christian; in their laws that's the way it was. But not him, he was coming to give testimony about love; it was his testimony and the Father's testimony; they were witnesses, not to condemn but to save. They were witnesses that didn't lie. But they condemned Jesus with false witnesses."

CHUCHU, Natalia's nephew, who is spending his vacation here: "He was coming to make humankind change; he wasn't coming to condemn anybody, and that's why he didn't want to condemn the adulterous woman. But at the end, even though he doesn't want to, he's going to judge, because not everybody's going to change and there's still going to be injustice in the world. Or better, love is going to judge. The ones who didn't feed the people, didn't give the people clothes and homes, those are the ones that love will judge and condemn."

OLIVIA: "In the Bible God has talked in his favor and in their consciences too he was testifying to what Jesus was saying. That's why Jesus says there are two witnesses."

I: "Jesus speaks here in a contradictory way: he doesn't judge and yet he does judge. It's the contradiction of love. Love wants humankind to be united, but the one who stands apart, love has to condemn him."

OSCAR: "It's because when people are united by love in a community, love is there already condemning the ones that reject that unity."

I: "This reminds me of something that Fidel said: that the tragedy of the revolution is that humankind had to be suppressed in order to be freed."

Then they asked him:
"Where is your Father?"
Jesus answered them:
"You do not know me or my Father;
if you knew me you would also know my
Father."

I: "That's peculiar, what he says. It seems that the logical thing would have been for him to say the opposite: that if they knew God they would have known him."

OSCAR: "Well, those people there, it seems like they didn't have any love among them. If they'd had love among themselves, they'd be knowing him, and therefore also his Father, which is the same thing as love."

OLIVIA: "Knowing him, or his message, is knowing God, because that's what God is: freedom. And rejecting the message of love is rejecting God."

BOSCO: "Jesus arrived like a political manifesto of God, and they didn't accept the manifesto. Then they couldn't know God because there wasn't any other shape."

OSCAR: "Man, Jesus came to this world, or was born from this world, which was all turned around, and he wanted to straighten it out, and that's why he says he knew where he was coming from and where he was going. And

that's why he says too that he's the Light.
Love is a fire and that fire had to burn all the
evil there is here. And it had to light the way
too."

WILLIAM: "Deep down he's telling them too
that when they reject humankind (what Jesus
was bringing was a new relation among people) they weren't knowing God."

I: "It's like saying that anyone who's a revolutionary knows God and anyone who's not a
revolutionary doesn't know God. They were
opposed to those changes he was bringing,
coming from one world and going to another
one. Those opposed to the changes aren't on
the side of God, because they're on the side of
injustice. They're in favor of darkness and not
light."

> *Jesus said these things in the temple,*
> *where the offering boxes were.*
> *But no one arrested him*
> *because his hour had not come.*

I: "It takes a lot of courage to say those
things right in the temple, the holiest place of
the Jews. And the Roman troops from the Antonia Tower were always keeping an eye on
the temple courtyards."

"He was inspired by love and he had no fear.
Besides, he had been sent by his Father. He
knew where he was coming from and where he
was going. He was going to death and also to
resurrection. And he gave us an example: at
the present time those in charge don't like to

hear what's said here, and we've got to say it."

OSCAR: "They believed in God but they didn't carry out God's law. They followed their own laws. And Christ set himself against their laws. That's what we must do. If we obey human laws, we're criminals."

LAUREANO: "The people were with him, and that's why they didn't dare arrest him."

8.

"The Truth Will Make You Free"

(John 8:31–47)

Then Jesus said to the Jews who had be-
  lieved in him:
"If you stick by what I tell you, you are truly
  my disciples;
and you will know the truth,
and the truth will make you free."

"He's talking all confused. Maybe the
things he's saying are too high up to be able
to understand them. That's why they told him
he was possessed, that is, neurotic," said
young JULIO GUEVARA.

MYRIAM, his sister: "But if he said those
things, it was so we could understand them."

ALEJANDRO: "He says the truth will make
us free, because the oppressors have con-
cealed reality from us. The truth that Christ
talks about is to uncover the injustice there is
in society, to show that there are social classes. Our eyes are opened and we see these
things. With lies we're deceived; we believe

it's proper to have rich and poor. When we understand reality, we liberate ourselves."

LAUREANO: "I believe the truth makes us free because the truth is equality. If we're all equal, we're free; if there's nobody who's bigger than the others, then we're free. Deceit is what enslaves us. They oppress with deceit, and we free ourselves with truth, unmasking the deceit."

FELIPE: "Truth teaches us that we're all equal, as Laureano says, and that all of us human beings must live a single reality, the reality that we're brothers and sisters. Not to look on anybody as master or slave, that seems to me the truth. The truth makes us brothers and sisters and therefore it frees us."

GLORIA: "I think it's clear. That's why they keep the poor in ignorance, because without ignorance you can't have exploitation."

I: "According to Jesus, it's not enough to believe in him, for the Gospel says he told those who 'had believed in him' that they would be his disciples only if they practiced what he said. It's only that praxis that gives us the truth, and therefore freedom. You can believe in Christ as the bourgeois Christians do, and that's not being a disciple, and that's not being free."

They answered him:
"We are children of Abraham
and we have never been slaves of anyone.
How do you say that we shall get to be free?"

*Jesus said to them: "I tell you the truth,
all those who sin are slaves of sin."*

I: "They claim they're free because they are
Israelites. According to the law the Israelites
could not be made slaves for life and were to
be treated as wage earners, since the whole
people had been freed by God from Egyptian
slavery. But that was a law that was merely
on paper."

FELIPE: "Maybe those Jews had a freedom
like the freedom they say we have, but the
freedom around here is freedom to abuse us,
freedom to exploit us all they can. It's freedom to sin, that is, to commit injustice, and
that's not freedom, it's oppression."

OSCAR: "You think you're free because
you're free to go anywhere you want with an
empty belly. It used to be that slaves worked
just for food, now it's the same; if you work
you use up your energy for a few pennies. Oppression has really got you shafted."

WILLIAM: "But where there's masters and
slaves nobody's free. That's why Jesus tells
the makers of oppression that they are slaves
of their sin, oppression."

I: "Yahweh in the Bible appears as the God
of Freedom, the God that brought Israel out
of Egypt; and he's a God that doesn't force
anyone even to worship him since he doesn't
want images; he only forces you to be free,
and he doesn't tolerate any image that makes
people subjects. That's the freedom that
Christ says his truth will give us. And that's
the only commandment that he brings, what

the Apostle Saint James calls: 'the law of freedom.' "

A slave is not always part of the family,
but a son is always part of the family.
If the Son gives you freedom, you will be
*   truly free.*

MANUEL: "If we agree to a system of deceit and exploitation, we're slaves. If we struggle for the establishment of justice on earth, we're children of God, and we're brothers and sisters of the others. We all make up a single family, with God and the others."

LAUREANO: "I believe Jesus Christ is saying that as long as some people are more powerful than others, there have to be slaves. And we're no longer brothers and sisters but masters and slaves."

I: "He's telling them that they'll be driven out of the house if they stay in the slave category, because slaves don't belong to the family. But he adds that the Son has authority equal to the authority of the Father, to give freedom to the slaves of the house, if the slaves agree to be free. It seems to be about a house where they're trying to emancipate the slaves."

BOSCO: "And he's telling them they can be part of a community with the Father, the family of the Trinity, but not until we're free."

They said to him:
"We are not bastard children;

> *we have only one Father,*
> *who is God."*

I: "They tell Jesus that they're not sons of whores. The prophets have talked a lot about the prostitutions of Israel: She was the wife of God but she was an adulterous wife. And they understand also that Jesus is telling them that their father is the devil."

OSCAR: "Their father must be the one that never tells the truth and keeps the people deceived and controls them by means of dictators. So the people are at ease, not knowing that they are his slaves, and so they don't worry."

> *Jesus said to them:*
> *"If God were your Father,*
> *you would love me,*
> *because I came from God,*
> *and I come on his behalf.*
> *I have not come on my own account;*
> *it was God who sent me.*
> *Why can't you understand what I say to you?*
> *Because you do not want to listen to my message."*

I: "He doesn't come by himself; he has been sent by the community of God, as Bosco says, by the communism of God, so that all people can form part of that communism. That is his message. And it's curious that he says they *can't* understand him because they *don't want to* hear him."

OSCAR: "The ones that can't understand, it seems to me, are the ones that don't want to be even with everyone but to be on top of the rest, so they don't want to hear: Screwing all the rest is what they want to be doing."

MANUEL: "He knows they're going to kill him; he feels himself among enemies. And it's because he brings liberation and they want to preserve injustice. It seems to me that's what it means when it says he died for our sins."

FELIPE: "Those jerks that thought they were saved because they were of the people of Abraham are like the exploiters of today who think they are saved because they belong to some religion."

> *Your father is the devil;*
> *you belong to him, and you want to do what*
>   *he wants.*
> *The devil has been a murderer from the be-*
>   *ginning.*

FELIPE: "I think it's a good thing to make it clear that the devil here isn't that ghost that people imagine and that suddenly comes out to scare you. The devil is a reality: he's self-ishness; he's the evil ideas you have about other people."

BOSCO: "But the devil is also a ghost, because the evil we now see going on in the politics of Nicaragua and other countries is a false reality: it's a ghost."

I: "The Apostle Saint James says something like what Felipe says: when somebody is tempted, the one that tempts him is his own selfishness. In the Bible 'Satan' means simply 'adversary.' Christ says this adversary is responsible for all the crimes and injustices of humanity, from the first murder (of Abel): because he's been a murderer from the beginning."

OLIVIA: "The murders of so many undernourished children or sick people that die for lack of medical attention, or those others that get murdered, all that's the action of the devil. There's still a lot of the devil in Nicaragua. It's the same kind of people that wanted to murder Jesus, and that he fought against."

DONALD: "Well, that devil can have a secret agent in any country, doing the work that he wants, carrying out all his orders. That's when there's a dictator, and all the people live doing what just one guy wants, the guy that's in charge."

I: "The devil, the adversary, is the force opposed to evolution. He is equal to oppression. According to Christ exploitation is murder."

He has never been based on truth,
and he never tells the truth.
When he tells lies he speaks of what comes
    out from inside him;
because he is a liar and is the father of lying.

BOSCO: "This applies exactly to the United States, just as if he'd seen it: its terrible crimes accompanied by lies, the propaganda of its radios."

"And this applies to Nicaragua just as if he'd lived at this time. Hasn't this regime been a murderer from the beginning, when the father of lying began it with the murder of Sandino the liberator?"

ALEJO: "Crime always goes with lying, because if it wasn't for propaganda, you wouldn't have injustice."

ELVIS: "Promising the people all kinds of things and not giving them anything and exploiting them more, that's the work of the devil too, the father of lying."

OSCAR: "They force the poor man to vote and the next day they forget about him and afterwards for any reason at all, bang, he's in jail. They don't care about anything! We mustn't let them fool us. And we've got to talk to the others, clear up their minds that they've got fooled. I can't explain myself, that's the truth, but you understand what I mean."

I: "Jesus identifies the devil, the adversary, with lying, because he's the adversary of truth. Lying and oppression are the same thing, just as truth and liberty are the same."

When I speak the truth you do not believe
  me.
Who among you can accuse me of a sin?
And if I speak the truth, why do you not
  believe me?

OLIVIA: "Evil has had more power than good, even though good is going to triumph in the end. At present, evil is bigger than good. And they didn't believe Jesus because he was speaking the truth, and all they believe is lies. If he'd spoken their lie, they sure would have believed him. The same thing is happening now."

"Why should they believe, if a guy that tells the truth gets his mouth shut up with a bullet, and that's that! That's the way it happens in Nicaragua, and that time the Sandinistas had to seize a radio station in Managua to tell the truth, and the government got so mad that they screwed the owner of the station for no reason. That's the way it happened in Christ's time, and because he told the truth he died."

WILLIAM: "Truth and justice are the same, as we've seen. Jesus says he speaks the truth because in him there's no injustice (no one can accuse him of a sin). His message is only about justice. Truth is reality and lying is false ideas with which people disfigure reality, and those ideas are produced by exploitation."

ELVIS: "He asks why they won't believe him when he tells them the truth but immediately afterwards, he tells why it is."

He who is from God listens to the words of
    God;
but as you are not from God, therefore you
    won't listen.

FELIPE: "The ones that are from God are the needy, the poor. The ones that the Father gave to Christ are the poor, right? Those of us that need everything and need everybody and want unity, *we* are the children of God."

WILLIAM: "The children of God are the ones that are on the side of justice, and they're the ones that listen to the message. The others 'won't listen,' because what they want is lying and crime."

IVAN: "Does that mean that not all people are children of God?"

LAUREANO: "The exploiters aren't children of God."

9.

The Good Samaritan

(Luke 10:25–37)

*A teacher of the law stood up and said to
   him,*
to lay a trap for him:
"Master, what must I do to win eternal life?"

I said it had always interested me that the
Gospel should say that that question was to
lay a trap for him.

MANUELITO: "They believed in a heap of religious rules, and they wanted to see if Jesus
said they had to follow them; if he said they
didn't, he set himself against the law."

ALEJANDRO: "It seems to me that what was
happening then with the law is happening
now with the Gospel: The law was extremely
clear, but they didn't understand it, and according to them, they were following it. And
they hope that Jesus will speak against the
law, as they understand it, so they can condemn him."

I: "I see. It's as if a supporter of this regime

should ask us what we think of the Gospels. That could be a dangerous question, couldn't it?"

ALEJANDRO: "It's all alike, it's the very same thing. Besides, they ask the question, they're always asking it."

LAUREANO: "He could have said: 'Take from the rich what they have and distribute it among the poor,' but that would have been dangerous."

> *Jesus answered him:*
> *"What is it that is written in the law?*
> *How do you read it?"*
> *The teacher of the law answered:*
> *"Love the Lord your God with all your heart,*
> *   with all your soul,*
> *with all your strength and with all your*
> *   mind;*
> *and love your neighbor as you love your-*
> *   self."*

LAUREANO: "In trying to catch Jesus in a trap, he was the one who fell into the trap. Jesus makes him say things he doesn't do."

Another: "Maybe he wanted to argue with him about worship in the temple, the sabbath, unclean food, purification, and many other laws that were nonsense, and Jesus makes him say what's important: loving God and your neighbor."

> *But he, trying to defend himself, said to Jesus: "And who is my neighbor?"*

I said that "neighbor," the nearby person, was applied in the Bible to all who were from Israel. Why would he ask who is his neighbor "trying to defend himself"?

ALEJANDRO: "Maybe because he realizes that he had never loved his neighbor. He could pray to God all he wanted and tell him that he loved him; but neighbor, shit, up to then he didn't even know who he was."

OLIVIA: "He didn't know his neighbor because he didn't have love. He did like they do nowadays: give a little alms, a bit of bread to a few poor children."

REBECA: "Maybe he loved his children, his close friends, but that was a selfish love; you can't call that love, because if you love just a tiny few, when there's all that enormous crowd of people, you're not loving anything."

FELIPE: "He knew very well who his neighbor was, but he didn't want Jesus to realize that he had asked the question to catch him in a trap."

OLIVIA: "Your neighbors are all of humanity, that's what that fellow didn't know, that his neighbors were everybody."

ALEJANDRO: "He thought they were the people who lived across the street, who surely were well-to-do like him."

We read the parable. A man was assaulted by thieves and left wounded on the road. A priest and a Levite passed by. A Samaritan took care of him and took him to an inn.

"Well, then, which of those three does it seem to you

*was the neighbor of the man assaulted by the
   thieves?"
The teacher of the law said:
"The one who took pity on him."
Then Jesus said to him:
"Go you and do the same."*

OLIVIA: "He gave him as an example a person of another race and another religion so
we can know that everybody is a neighbor. He
gave as an example one who wasn't a neighbor but just the opposite, an enemy."

FELIPE: "The man's question was what did
you have to do to win eternal life, true life,
and Jesus' answer is: love. Love is life."

An old man from San Miguelito: "But the
law talks about love of God and love of neighbors, not just love of neighbors."

FELIPE: "But love of neighbors is the same
as the other love, and that's the only example
he gives."

MANUEL: "It seems to me, according to this
example of the religious and the heretic, that
love of neighbors is more important, because
some take care of the temple but not of neighbors, and so they are evil, and the other one
didn't take care of the temple; he was a heretic, and he was the good one."

I: "It seems to me that you could say it this
way: those who love God without loving their
neighbor are not carrying out the law, but
they are carrying out the law if they love
their neighbor without loving God. Jesus tells
the teacher of the law to do as the Samaritan
does."

Another: "Those people in the temple really didn't love God because they didn't love their neighbor, and as we see, the law of the two loves is a single law. Those were only religious people; they devoted themselves only to their prayers. So perhaps maybe that's why they didn't stop on the road, because they were in a hurry to get to their temple duties. It was religion itself that prevented them from loving their neighbor, and that kind of thing is still going on."

I: "But we're accustomed to thinking that this parable is to make us see that the Samaritan is the one who loved his neighbor, and what Jesus asks at the end of the parable is which of the three who passed by on the road *was the neighbor* of the wounded man."

One answered: "The man without religion was the neighbor."

"It wasn't the wounded man?"

"It wasn't the wounded man."

MANUEL: "It's confused, because he said: 'Love your neighbor,' and here it appears it's somebody else."

FELIPE: "It seems that instead it's the one who serves that's the neighbor."

LAUREANO: "O.K., but notice that if somebody serves me and I serve him, we're neighbors."

I said there's been so much talk of neighborly love that we no longer know clearly what the phrase means. Among us there's a more up-to-date word for "neighbor" that means the same thing. It's "comrade." The law spoke of loving your comrade as you loved yourself, and the scribe asks who the comrade is. And at the end of the parable, when Jesus asked who was the comrade of the wounded man, he had to admit that it was "the one who took pity on him."

"It's clearer that way, saying comrade instead of neighbor."

And I said the truth was that the two are comrades, the Samaritan and the wounded man, for comrades have to be two. The term "neighbor" we must then understand as a mutual relation: he is neighbor to me and I am neighbor to him.

"Yes, because being charitable to the poor, giving them worn-out clothes, isn't loving your neighbor. Love of your neighbor is comradeship. Because that man not only cared for the wounded man but he took him to a hotel and paid for his room and said he'd pay for anything extra when he came back and, of course, from then on they remained friends; they were already comrades."

LAUREANO: "The people are the wounded man who's bleeding to death on the highway. The religious people who are not impressed by the people's problems are those two that were going to the temple to pray. The atheists who are revolutionaries are the good Samaritan of the parable, the good companion, the good comrade."

"The lesson is that everybody must be our neighbor, our companion, and that there should be no barriers between us."

"We're all neighbors."

"But Jesus doesn't say that. Jesus asks: 'Of the three, which one was the neighbor of the wounded man?' Does he mean that the others weren't, the priest and the Levite?"

"They weren't."

"Because those guys didn't love."

And the man from San Miguelito insisted: "Neighbors are the whole human race."

MANUEL: "Where there's mutual aid, that's where there's neighbors. Only where there's comradeship, where there's companions and comrades, there's neighbors."

"Jesus makes it clear that some, because they're selfish, stop being neighbors of the others."

I: "There's something else that's strange in this Gospel. The scribe has said what the commandment is: 'Love the Lord your God with all your heart,' and so forth, 'and love your neighbor as you love yourself,' and Jesus has told him that he has answered well. But then Jesus gives only the example of love of your neighbor, a pagan who comes to the aid of the wounded man, and he says to the scribe: 'Go and do the same.' We might wonder: and the commandment about the love of God, what about that? Because to illustrate the double commandment Jesus might have given the example of a priest who is going to the temple to fulfill all his duties in the worship of God, and on the way he helps the wounded man. If anybody now should give, as an example of the love 'of God and neighbor' an atheistic Marxist, a Che Guevara, who loved only his neighbor, wouldn't we find this incongruous?"

ALEJANDRO: "And the Christian, the one who goes to the temple, is left looking silly! Do you suppose Jesus accepted the first commandment, because it was written in the law, so as not to get involved in problems, but he wanted to show that the important thing was the other thing?"

ELVIS: "The fact is that in your neighbor there's God. It's not that love of God gets left out, it's that those who love their neighbor are right there loving God."

ALEJANDRO: "It's too bad that boob didn't go on asking, because now they lay the same trap for us, and they tell us that stuff about the Samaritan is all very well, but that what's most important is the spiritual part, religion, the love of God. And if he'd asked more questions, this would have come out clearer."

LAUREANO: "The other poor bastards are loving something that doesn't exist."

I said that Jesus really was clear enough, but his words have been interpreted in a way that makes them unclear. He teaches somewhere else that the most important commandment is to do unto others as we want them to do unto us. The Apostle Saint James will say later that to love your neighbor as you love yourself is "the supreme commandment," and Saint Paul will say that the whole law consists of love of your neighbor. It's true that the law said, as the scribe has said:

"Love the Lord your God with all your heart, with all your soul, with all your strength and with all your mind," but in the Bible it says that this is because Yahweh is the one who freed the Jews from Egypt and he is the only one who does justice to the poor and the oppressed. It's like saying that you don't need to have any God except human love and justice. That's why Jesus somewhere else says that the second commandment is "like the first," and in this parable he shows that the two are fulfilled by fulfilling the second. And that's why too, when the rich young man asks him what he should do to be saved, Jesus quotes to him the commandments about neighborly love, without mentioning the one about love of God.

LAUREANO: "In other words, he's saying that there is no God, then, that God is your neighbor."

I: "He's saying that God is love."

LAUREANO: "He's saying that to love others, that's God."

I: "He's saying that there *is* a God but God is that."

LAUREANO: "God's all of us, then."

I: "Love. All, but united; not all separated, hating each other or exploiting each other. It's really not all of us, because those two who passed by there, they weren't neighbors of the other one. If we have a meeting here in which there are exploiters and murderers, you're not going to say: 'God is all of us.' "

LAUREANO: "God is all of us who love each

other. And all of us who don't love each other
and are screwing the people, that's the devil."

I: "Saint Augustine says God is the love
with which we love each other."

ALEJANDRO: "What has been said here is
very important!"

OLIVIA: "As I see it, we mustn't try to love
God, because God doesn't exist, as Laureano
says; God's in heaven and is not asking us
for anything for himself here on earth. Some
say they love him, but forget it; they love
him because they don't see him. There are
people who prefer to love the God of heaven,
because they're not seeing him. It's hard to be
a Christian, like that Samaritan was. It's
easier to be just religious, like so many
Catholics are, and be praying to God in the
temple."

I: "When they judged Jesus the main accusation against him was that he was against
the temple. A Samaritan woman, another
heretic, asked him if the temple of Jerusalem
was the true one, and he answered her that
now God wasn't going to be adored in temples
but everywhere 'in spirit and in truth.' Since
then we Christians have filled the earth with
temples, but Jesus taught us that the only
temple is the human being. The man fallen by
the wayside in Jerusalem, he was the temple."

Another: "The government likes to have
sermons just about the love of God, about the
salvation of the soul, and about heaven. I believe they even pay for those radio sermons.

That gringo preacher, Spencer, who preaches every day sweetly about the spiritual salvation of Christ, he's probably a CIA agent."

A South American hippie: "But our enemies are also part of God, because they're also human beings. If they do evil it's maybe because they're mistaken, and we must love them."

I said we must love them and fight them to free them from the injustice they are committing. God is not in the one who is being selfish; it's the devil who's in him, as Laureano says. God is only in the one who loves. God is probably in the exploiters when they aren't exploiting any more and are united with us. There are some people in the parable we haven't spoken about: the assailants. These are the exploiters, who have legally assaulted the people, with the laws that they themselves have made, and they have left the people naked and covered with wounds, bleeding to death at the wayside of history.

LAUREANO: "And while religion went along that road without looking at the wounded man, communism, which didn't believe in God, has been the good companion that took up the wounded man and took him to a shelter where he could have food and a roof and clothing and medicine, all free."

10.

Martha and Mary

(Luke 10:38–42)

At the hut. We have had rice, black beans, fish, and avocados. Teresita and Doña Justa cooked. Juan, who is four, is playing, kicking a big ball around among us, while we talk.

Jesus came to a little town and stayed at the home of Martha and Mary. Martha was very busy with her household tasks and Mary sat at Jesus' feet to listen to him. And Martha said to Jesus:

> *"Lord, doesn't it matter to you at all*
> *that my sister leaves me alone with all the*
>   *work?*
> *Tell her to help me."*
> *But Jesus answered:*
> *"Martha, Martha, you are concerned and af-*
>   *flicted by many things,*
> *but only one is necessary."*

"It seems that Martha didn't understand what concerned Mary ."

"Martha was certainly concerned about cooking a chicken for lunch, and Mary wasn't helping."

OLIVIA: "Well, Mary didn't give food much importance. She thought teaching was more important than cooking. After listening to that teaching, they had time enough to get that chicken ready. The same thing can apply to us. On many Sundays we aren't interested in coming here because we have things to do and we're cooking our dinner. That means we're not interested in the community, what's most important."

TOMAS: "Martha was getting ready to cook, but Mary knew that he was the word of God, which is food. Am I right? There are some who don't come here because they have to take care of the pigs, to look at the cornfields, to fish. All that's all right, but what's more important is the word of God: That's necessary. Martha was doing that for love of him, but Mary was doing something better, which was to hear his word, which was love. And hearing his word, they could learn to love the others, to serve them."

OSCAR: "Then he wasn't hungry; he just wanted to talk, and he wouldn't have minded sleeping on the floor. Martha was worrying about trifles, with Jesus right there, instead of profiting from his words!"

CESAR: "It wasn't right to be cooking that meal to celebrate his coming and to entertain him, and to lose his teachings because she was cooking. The best part there could be was to listen to him. But Christ doesn't want people to forget about food and necessities on account of his teachings."

ALEJANDRO: "He'd said we should seek justice and everything else would come with it. It's important to concern ourselves about other people's food, everybody's food, and that's just what justice is. But that's not the same thing as being concerned about going to cook a lunch, because that's not important. What she was really doing was only entertaining him, and meanwhile maybe Mary was talking about very interesting subjects with him, talking maybe about food for all the people, and other problems about people's lives that were going to get solved, medicine, talking about how to change the world. And Martha, concerned only about that meal, was being very silly up to a certain point."

"I think what Jesus wanted to say to this Martha was that it's more important to be at the meeting, talking back and forth, about the problems of economic or spiritual life or whatever, and not be preparing meals. Lots of people on Sunday stay away from coming here to do their chores, picking up four sticks of wood maybe, and not giving any heed to the community meetings."

OSCAR: "It seems Martha was pretty selfish. She was more concerned about those chores, but she wanted Mary to be with her too, and not to be doing something better, listening about these things that are very important for us. And if I stay home, how am I going to know what we're saying here?"

"Lots of us are interested in what we're going to eat on Monday. Getting ready what we're going to eat tomorrow. Or even this evening."

"Concerning yourself with Christ is also concerning yourself with dinner. The fact is that since she's concerned only about those in her own household, her attitude is selfish."

"Martha was concerned only about Christ."

"About Christ, without thinking about all the Christs of today," added OLIVIA. "It's like I'm here waiting on Ernesto, cooking, concentrating on him, ignoring the rest, the community."

MARIA: "One was concerned only about the little group, and the other about everyone, about the kingdom, about all of humanity."

OSCAR: "What was happening to Martha, I figure, is that she was selfish. She would have worked and would have been content, and I think that then she would have taken part in some of what Jesus was saying too, what he was saying to Mary, then and there, the whole group. She was envious. Martha should have done her cooking and let the sister tell her everything afterwards. But she didn't want Mary to be there. Let her be working with her! You see? And then that's where she kind of shit on her."

"It's like Olivia, for example, who has a lot of kids, and it's up to her to come and cook on

Sundays. And she'd like to have everybody there with her, and maybe we're solving our problems here, and she didn't care, she didn't want the girls to take part. That's being selfish. A woman that's only interested in food, that's the way Martha was, then."

OLIVIA: "I think she said it out of simplicity. She was generous. Look, you ought to see what it's like to be stuck in a kitchen. I think he gave that lesson to make us see that food shouldn't prevent us from being interested in the kingdom. Because meals come at any hour. We've got supper ready right now."

OSCAR: "Then you're like Martha."

"I say that the two of them were acting all right, but one was doing more important work than the other. Martha was working on material food, and Mary was doing a spiritual work."

I: "Jesus doesn't exactly make a distinction between material and spiritual work. He just says that Martha is concerned about 'many things' and that 'only one is necessary.' "

OSCAR: "Man, I think it's unity."

ALEJANDRO: "It's quite clear they were talking about solving problems on the social level, and Martha was trying to solve practical problems. How were they going to cook the chicken for that day's lunch and the others were talking about solving the problems of the world."

"It seems to me that what's necessary is unity, equality among everybody; the problem of the relations among people, that's what it was important to talk about. Martha was concerned about problems that are many but not important."

I: "We might say, then, that what Jesus is saying here is that the only important thing is love."

OSCAR: "From love comes unity, right?"

OLIVIA: "And having unity, we all eat. Where there's love there's food for everybody, but where there's no love there's food only for some families, not for all. The only important thing, then, was that thing she was talking over with Jesus."

Mary has chosen the better part,
and no one is going to take it away from her.

"Nobody can take away love."

"Love is what's important, not food and the other things."

"You really have to distinguish between food for a private house, which is what Martha was preparing, and food for everybody. The only thing necessary is love between everybody."

OSCAR: "But look, Ernesto, the way I understand it is that you can find food anywhere but you can't find love very easily; and that thing, love, is what Mary was looking for; she wanted to have love and she wasn't interested in food. She'd forgotten to think about lunch, and not until Martha came to scold her did she remember and she got flustered, but Jesus said: There's no need to

get flustered; she's devoted to more important work. Food, I can eat any old thing. But
what's important for me is that there's a bit
of love in my heart. And I have to find out
how to acquire it, and I have to look for
unity."

"Mary chose the best part. And so was
Martha's the worst part?"

"It would be an average one."

"It seems Martha wanted to take that part
from Mary, and Jesus tells her that nobody's
going to take it away from her."

"And that part nobody's going to take away
from her; instead she's going to share it with
everybody."

"Mary, even though she wasn't helping her
sister and wasn't being nice to her, there at
Jesus' feet she was united with all of us."

TOMAS: "And Mary chose the best part because from having been listening to his word
she was going to follow him and afterward
she was going to be with him always."

OSCAR: "That's pretty clear."

I: "Traditionally in these two figures contemplation and action have been represented.
But you have found a somewhat different interpretation, and it seems to me better suited
to the text."

WILLIAM: "Couldn't we sum it up this
way: one was a revolutionary and the other
wasn't?"

11.

Riches

(Luke 12:13–21)

One among the people said to Jesus:
"Master, tell my brother to give me my part
of the inheritance."
But Jesus said to him:
"Man, who put me between you like a judge
or a divider?"

I: "Didn't Jesus do badly by not wanting to do justice between those two?"

FELIPE: "He was coming to teach us love. If people carried out his teaching, the brother wouldn't steal the inheritance of the brother."

WILLIAM: "He didn't come to distribute the riches; it's up to society to do that. And the sharing ought to be done among everybody, not just between two. In that sharing they asked Jesus to do, the rest were left out. They ask him to sanction private property, the inheritance laws, the status quo. He refuses, he hasn't come for that. On the contrary, he's come to destroy that social order."

One of the Guevara girls: "I ask you: would it be right for that man to get that money?"

LAUREANO: "First you have to find out if that inheritance was large or small. If it was small and he was poor, it certainly would be right. If it was a lot of money, no."

ALEJANDRO: "It was probably a lot, because it seems he comes to Jesus seeking the intervention of an important person for a very important question. And Jesus right there talks about riches, about rich people, so it seems it's a matter of a big capital."

OSCAR: "Well, if that's so, it wasn't right, because it was asking Jesus to be a capitalist, to be an exploiter, to have too much; and that doesn't do any good to anybody, to have too many things. That way Jesus would have done him harm."

TOMAS: "It's clear that Jesus did right in not wanting to divide up that wealth. If he'd told Jesus he was going to divide it among everybody, maybe Jesus would have gone along, but there it was just going to be among two rich people."

LAUREANO: "He didn't come to divide up wealth, to create capital. Many rich people think religion is for that, to defend their private property, their inheritances. It seems to me that in a Christian society, that's to say, in a socialist or communist society, there shouldn't be any inheritance."

OSCAR: "That man was asking for money, which was going to isolate him from the other brothers and sisters. In fighting for *his* inheritance, only thinking about himself, he

was getting separated from other people.
That money was going to make him poor, because true wealth isn't money, it's love. That
man didn't know that riches are other people."

And I said that this reminded me of a
phrase of Marx: The greatest wealth is the
other person, and that it's poverty that
makes one feel that need for the greater
wealth.

"These words of Jesus give the impression
that he answered in anger. He was probably
sore. How could they think he was coming to
solve questions of money, to have somebody
get a half million pesos!"

"He wants nothing to do with the rich, not
even to do justice among them, because he
knows that among them everything is injustices, and he rejects their system totally."

"He hasn't come to earth to divide inheritance, because who said that inheritors have
a right to receive their inheritance?"

"The man saw that Jesus was just and
that's why he wants to set him up as a judge.
But he didn't know that Jesus' justice was
another kind of justice, revolutionary justice.
Even now there are Christians who think
that Christ's justice is the justice of capitalism. The Chilean military junta says it's
restoring Christianity, because it's restoring
private property."

FELIPE: "Jesus was coming to divide all the
wealth of the world among all the people."

A Protestant from the opposite shore: "It

seems to me he wasn't coming to share material things but spiritual things, and this man wanted him to share material things."

OLIVIA: "Well, it seems to me he comes to share material things too, but not just to two people. Because notice that just with spiritual things, forgetting material things, you can't live. And the spiritual and the material can't be separated; it has to be one single united thing, but not shared just between two people. Because notice that if the only thing shared is spiritual, then the people starve to death."

FELIPE: "If you want to achieve a spiritual life, you have to achieve it through material things. Because if I love God ('I'm on the side of God!'), to prove it I have to do something for my comrades and share what I have, be brothers and sisters with everyone. If I don't achieve it in material things, I'm not loving; it's more like I'm hating."

Notice and beware of all greed;
for people's lives do not depend on the many
things they may have.

OLIVIA: "Happiness doesn't depend on riches. There are many rich people that are unhappy."

MARIITA: "It's the riches that make them unhappy. They have worries we don't have."

I: "According to Jesus, it's not just happiness; it's life itself that doesn't depend on the things one may have."

TOMAS: "A selfish person is dead in the midst of life."

MARCELINO: "Life depends on food, clothing, also housing, medicine. But he says not 'on the many things they may have': that's to be rich."

FELIPE: "The many things (having too much), that's what kills life."

REBECA, Marcelino's wife: "The fact that some people have too much of a lot of things, that makes for law suits, wars, that also kill life."

WILLIAM: "He's also saying that life doesn't depend on *having;* it depends on *being.*"

TERESITA: "So that's why he didn't want to give that man the riches he was fighting for, they aren't any good."

LAUREANO: "As I understand it, he says that having riches isn't living, it's being isolated, it's death."

OLIVIA: "He shows that riches are the same as greed. Because he talks about riches and before he said 'beware of greed.' Because the richer you are the greedier you have to be. And then it's death, not happiness; so riches are a curse."

ALEJANDRO: "Riches that are shared unevenly."

DONALD: "Here he was showing the one who was asking him this that he shouldn't be selfish. Because he *was* being selfish. He wouldn't let the brother alone who had the things. And then, instead of abandoning that system, he wanted to be another greedy man, or he'd become one. They'd be two greedy men fighting over an inheritance."

Then he gave them this example:
There was a rich man,
and his lands gave a great harvest.
And he thought:
"I know what I'm going to do:
I'm going to tear down my barns
and build other bigger ones,
and in them I'll keep all my harvests and all
*   my goods*
and I'll say to myself:
'My friend, you have many things stored up
*   for many years;*
rest, eat, drink, and be merry.' "
But God said to him:
"Fool, this very night you will die,
and all you have stored up, who will get it?"
That's what happens to the man that piles
*   up riches for himself,*
but who is poor in the eyes of God.

FELIX: "That rich man, when he dies he's not saved, because he was poor in love; he wasn't rich in God's view. And others enjoy the riches."

I: "Jesus gives the example of a rich man who died when he had the most riches and other people enjoyed his riches. And then he says *that's* what happens to all those who pile up for themselves. But that was an example."

OLIVIA: "The rich man is dead now, because he's selfish, and he's not enjoying his riches."

FELIPE: "The guy that has riches doesn't have love, so he's poor in the eyes of God, because God is love among brothers and sisters."

TOMAS: "That rich guy was selfish because all he thought about was making his barns bigger to store up more just for himself. That's what all the rich always do."

LAUREANO: "No doubt about it; those who store up riches when there's so many people to share with are already damned; they're damned for storing things up."

ALEJANDRO: "What the man in the parable did is what rich people do now: Keep the money in the bank and take it easy. They eat and drink and have fun like that man. They live in an endless fiesta. And they go on accumulating more, they go on exploiting and living happily off the work of the others. Like that man in the Gospel: because that man by himself couldn't have gathered all those harvests that wouldn't fit into his barns, he did it with the labor of others."

REBECA: "The bad part about wealth is that it makes them poor in God's eyes, poor in love."

OLIVIA: "And they're very unfortunate in the eyes of God, because the richer a man is, the more he has exploited. And then he owes all that money, that sweat that he's stolen from the worker. Some are poorer than others in the eyes of God, and the richest are the poorest in God's eyes."

"The richest one is the one who's devoted

himself to screwing others, so he's the worst for the poor people, so he's the poorest in God's eyes."

"The ones that are the most miserable (those that are most lacking in love) are the ones that have the most riches."

"But Jesus speaks of the one that 'piles up riches for himself.' He's not against big harvests, he's against piling them up just for yourself. Like that man did: to keep them and rest and enjoy himself the rest of his life."

"Neither of the two sons-of-bitches had a right to that inheritance; all of it was the people's money. Just as it was everybody's wealth that man wanted to store in his barns. Who says he could enjoy all by himself that great harvest, if he didn't harvest it all by himself."

"And even less inherit it."

12.

The Good Servant
and the Evil Servant

(Luke 12:41–46)

Then Peter asked Jesus:
"Lord, did you give this example just for us,
or for everybody?"

I: "What Jesus has previously said is that
we have to be prepared, and that the Son of
Man would come like a thief in the night.
Peter asks him if he's saying that for everybody or only for the apostles. Jesus doesn't
answer him directly; he gives him another
example: a master that goes away and leaves
a servant in charge of his property. This can
be a good servant who has charge of the other
servants."

But if that servant thinks his master will be
late in coming,
and he begins to mistreat the other servants
and the maids,

and begins to eat and get drunk,
then his master will return when least ex-
  pected,
and at an hour not announced;
and he will give him the most terrible pun-
  ishment,
condemning him to suffer the same fate as
  the infidels.

I: "Why is it that Christ doesn't answer Peter directly but gives him another example? And what did he mean by that example?"

GIGI: "First we must ask ourselves who the master is, and what it is that he leaves his servant charged with, and then we might see if it applies to everyone or is only for some. Isn't the master Christ, and also the people at the same time?"

I: "Maybe it can be explained this way: the Christ that is leaving is an individual person, and the Christ that is returning is the people. In other Gospel passages we've seen that the return of the Son of Man will come when he comes back as the people."

GIGI: "I believe that what Christ has left in our charge is history, humanity's evolutionary progress toward a just society. There are people who work for this revolution and who worry about it, and there are people who oppose it by exploiting, mistreating their neighbors."

I: "What Gigi says is quite right. But I think Jesus is referring here to the hierarchy of his church. Peter has asked him, and he asks him,

in the name of the hierarchy, if he's referring
to them. Jesus answers that there are good
and evil administrators. The evil ones are the
ones who think the master is going to be late
in coming and who mistreat the other servants and devote themselves to feasts and
sprees. In the Gospel according to Saint
Matthew it says that they 'drink with the
drunkards.' It's not that they are really
drunk but that they're celebrating with the
drunkards."

GIGI: "It's clear that he's referring to the
church leaders who attend the parties of the
bourgeoisie, the exploiters."

FELIPE: "It seems to me that Jesus gave
that example for the leaders; it refers to the
leaders, whether they're the church leaders
or the political leaders. Why make this distinction? And what God leaves to all his servants are the material possessions that we
have in life, all the riches of the earth, that
ought to be divided up among everybody and
that nobody ought to be deprived of. But they
do deprive, the people that are living high
with banquets and parties and great feasts
and sprees in their clubs, all at the people's
expense, wasting and squandering among a
few people what belongs to everybody."

WILLIAM: "And that business about mistreating the other servants, that's repression, which always goes with exploitation."

I: "But I believe Jesus was thinking of the
leaders that he was leaving, the leaders of his
church. They've asked him if he's referring to

them specially or to everybody. With this example it seems to me that he's telling them: to you."

GIGI: "But as Felipe says, too, you can apply this to any leader in general."

I: "That Colombian cardinal and those Colombian bishops, for example, who are allied with the bourgeoisie; they get drunk with them, so to speak, though personally they may not drink much. They've just opposed a strike of bank clerks that was supported by a group of priests, and they've just applauded the repressive measures of the government, including the measures taken against those priests. They do that because they believe the coming of Christ is very far off and that the kingdom of God won't be until the next world. And Christ says at the end that they'll be treated like the infidels, the pagans; this is one more proof that he's talking to the people of his church. In Matthew it says the punishment that they'll receive is the punishment of the 'hypocrites.' To Christ the hypocrites are the Pharisees: this is another proof that he's talking to the religious leaders."

OSCAR: "When all of us, young and old, agree to fight against injustice, then Jesus begins to appear at the doors of the houses. When we don't want anybody anymore to be boss over anybody else but to have everybody equal, everybody the same, that's when Christ will be coming or is already come."

A worker: "It's hard to reach that point. If that's the way it is, that he won't come until then, it seems to me he'll never come, because that society of equality that he's talking about seems false to most people, everybody getting together like Jesus says."

OSCAR: "Those people that are opposed will be eliminated; that'll be the punishment he talks about here."

GLORIA: "So you think he's not going to come?"

The worker: "I don't say he's not going to come."

GLORIA: "That he's still not coming, you say."

OSCAR: "That new society can come at any moment, when least expected, and it can catch us by surprise."

I: "And therefore we have to be ready for that change that can come at any moment."

OSCAR: "When we talk about the second coming many of us have an idea that we're going to see Christ in person. I think we're seeing him right now. Every place we're seeing a social change, it's him coming and he's already coming to judge."

GIGI: "Two thousand years ago Christ gave us an idea of a society of love. It's very hard for this to happen suddenly, just as our comrade says. We're not all going to become good overnight. But since then lots of things have happened. We now have a social organization, socialism, which certainly didn't create for the first time the idea of love but it does give love a possible form among people. Humanity will have evolved a lot in the next two thousand years and we're going to have a really perfect society (but I don't believe it'll take two thousand years; it'll be much sooner). People who think there'll never be a just society, that people will never stop being selfish, they're the ones that are thinking that Christ is never coming, at least not in this world, in history."

DONALD: "But people who want the change *are* hoping for it."

I: "And why was it that Christ didn't answer Peter directly but did it with another example?"

ALEJANDRO: "Maybe he didn't tell him yes or no, because that way it could be applied to others, as Felipe has applied it. He gave an example that can be applied very directly to the apostles, but he didn't want to tell them: only to you. It's an example that can be applied to everybody that has social responsibilities; but he didn't want to take away from the apostles the great, the tremendous responsibility that they have."

I: "This could never have been understood clearly by just one of us. We've understood it very clearly all together. Any other comment?"

"Everything has been said."

13.

The Wedding Guests

(Luke 14:7–14)

From Managua, in a yacht, have come some fairly wealthy people and they are attending this Mass. Also present is young Dionisio, from the Communist Youth of Costa Rica.

We read that Jesus was invited to dinner in the home of an important Pharisee, and he saw how they quarrelled about the best seats. And he said:

When they invite you to a wedding party,
do not sit in the best seat,
for another guest more important than you
*   may arrive*
and the one who invited you both may come
*   to say to you:*
"Give your place to this man."
Then you will have to go in shame to take the
*   last seat.*
On the contrary, when they invite you,
sit in the last place,

so that when the one that invited you comes,
he will say to you: "My friend, come closer."

One of the young men of the commune (slyly): "It seems he's saying you mustn't be an exploiter but one of the exploited."

I: "The opposite of the exploiter isn't the exploited one but the revolutionary. He says we must be revolutionaries, and the revolutionary must take the place of the exploited, as long as society is divided into exploiters and exploited. And it's precisely from the exploited that freedom will come. And they will then occupy the first seats."

FELIPE: "He advises equality; everybody alike."

OSCAR: "He doesn't say equality; he says take the last seats."

LAUREANO: "It's the same as that other thing that Jesus said, when they asked him who was the most important, and he said the one who served. The one in the first place isn't most important."

I: "If everyone has a spirit of service to the others, there aren't any firsts or lasts and you reach the equality that Felipe is talking about."

CESAR: "In Cuba the millionaire sugar cutters have a very special place on the platform on the July 26 rallies. They're near Fidel because they're the ones that have worked the hardest. They're called 'millionaires' not because they have millions of pesos that they've taken from others but because they've cut more than a million arrobas of sugar cane; they're the ones who've given most to society. Just as in capitalist society the rich are in first place, there the most selfless workers are the ones in the place of honor."

FELIPE: "Here it's just the opposite."

LAUREANO: "That business about the millionaire cutters is because they've won the friendship of the people. It's the people that put you up there; you don't put yourself up there. Because I became like the people, that's why the people put me in this place. That's why Christ says that he's going to be taken from the last place and put in the first place."

OSCAR: "Or better, the ones that humble themselves, the people send them to the first place."

LAUREANO: "The ones that serve most."

OSCAR: "They are put at the head."

CESAR: "And this happens with the millionaire cutters, because the workers have always been at the low end of the table, and then comes the revolution and it gives the workers their right place. It takes them from the place where they put them and gives them the place they deserve, a place of honor."

So you will receive honors from those who
are seated at table with you.
Because he who is raised up will be humbled
and he who is humbled will be raised up.

FELIPE: "That's exactly what the revolution is: to flip the tortilla."

I: "And that is the subversion of the kingdom of heaven. 'Subvert' comes from the Latin *subvertere*, which means to put down what is up and up what is down."

ALEJANDRO: "It seems to me very important what the Gospel says here. I realized that everybody always wants to be the leader and to dominate. They want to be more important than others, and that's always a reason for division in the left: that everybody wants to be on top. And that's a selfish attitude. You think you're a revolutionary and you're really not being one. What you want is to dominate. What you want is power. Jesus saw that at that dinner, when he saw that everybody wanted the first seats."

> *When you give a lunch or a supper,*
> *do not invite your friends, or your brothers*
>   *and sisters,*
> *or your relatives, or your rich neighbors;*
> *because they in turn will invite you,*
> *and you will thus be repaid.*
> *On the contrary, when you give a party,*
> *invite the poor, the disabled, the lame, and*
>   *the blind.*

I: "He's talking to the rich. Because he says this to the one who invited him, and according to the Gospel, he was an important Pharisee. And he speaks to him of his 'rich neighbors.' And only a rich person can invite the rich."

"But a party with poor people, lame people, blind people, would that be joyful?"

MARCELINO: "It ought to be joyful."

TOMAS: "He advises this because then that rich man would be with God, because God is with the humble, and if he invites those people God is at his party, and that party is joyful."

I: "And the parties of the rich aren't joyful?"

OSCAR: "They're joyful for them, but they're not really joyful, because they're only among themselves. It's a selfish joy."

One of those who came on the yacht, a lawyer: "Let's not fall into demagoguery. If anyone gives a party it's to be joyful, to have a good time. And Christianity isn't opposed to joy. And let's be realistic: if I give a party and don't invite my friends but invite some beggars, that could be a work of charity but it's not fun, not a party. You mustn't take this literally."

MARCELINO: "And I'm not going to have fun at a party with other people that are not of my class, because they can't be my friends."

The lawyer: "Exactly."

MARCELINO: "But then he means there shouldn't be social classes, so that all of us can be capable of being friends and of being able to enjoy ourselves at the same party."

FELIPE: "It seems to me very good, what Jesus says to them here, and I think it not only refers to giving a party but to distributing everything among all the others, and the distribution ought to be made among the needy and not among people who already have and who don't need."

MANUELITO: "Yes, but the distribution shouldn't just be of material things, but of everything, because people have many other needs. And that's why he gives the example of a party; parties aren't just to satisfy hunger."

OLIVIA: "It's about the distribution of everything. The rich really do share their things with others, in their parties, their clubs, all the life they lead. They spend a lot of money among themselves, and they give each other gifts, and the money never leaves their group. And then Jesus tells them they ought to share with the poor, not share with the rich."

PANCHO: "Unfortunately we act that way, too. When we have a meeting, a lunch, anything, we also invite our closest friends, our best friends, and not others that maybe need that food more. That's very common among us."

ALEJANDRO: "We have to understand what a party is, what's the meaning. Because a party's not charity. To feed people I can simply cook a pile of food and give it to people that are hungry. But a party's something more than that, it's not just giving food, like we were saying. It's also something spiritual. There are elegant people and rich people that you can't get together with at a party because they don't have anything intelligent to say to you. I'd rather be in the midst of thinking, poor people like here—right?—than in the middle of elegant people, mental cripples, with shitty ideas, as we say, because you can't understand them. On the other hand, you can be in a very agreeable party spirit with drinks and food, with your people, with worthy people spiritually and ideologically. But parties shouldn't be charity. Those rich people that give a party from time to time for poor people, they're not doing anything, just putting a band-aid on misery. Some of them, on their birthday, they give a party for prisoners or old folks, but afterwards they go home to their houses to have a ball, the real party with other people."

I: "Jesus advises them to break with their families, with their circle of rich people, with their class. And the fact that they invite the poor to the party means that the poor stop being poor, and that in society everything is shared equally: health, clothing, culture. Because a party with crippled, sick, ignorant people isn't a very good party."

LAUREANO: "And sharing those things can't be done individually; we have to do it together, in a revolutionary society."

I: "In a revolutionary society, as Laureano says, or in a Christian one, which is the same, everyone will be seated at the banquet of life and abundance."

MARIITA: "For rich people names and family are very important, and that's why Jesus tells them the first thing they must do is break the family ties: don't invite 'your brothers and sisters,' 'your relatives.' "

FELIPE: "I still think, Ernesto, that this isn't a party. It's not really a party. As I said before, it's about sharing. Because the bosses, they do it among their relatives and friends and among those of their social class. And Jesus says how they must do it."

DIONISIO: "The fact that a rich man gives parties for the poor is very bad: it means that there's somebody that has enough for everybody and there are others who don't have anything. And there wouldn't be any need for anyone to give alms, if they hadn't taken the workers' wages away from them. What's needed is not for the rich to give more alms but for the poor, by organizing themselves, to make poverty disappear. And sharing the wealth of a society, it should be not just with the elite; everybody should come in on it; that's the basis of a revolutionary society. We mustn't imitate what the rich do, in the selfish enjoyment of their wealth. And the most important conclusion, as the other comrades have already said, is that we must struggle so that there'll be an equal enjoyment of all the wealth."

TOMAS: "When there's no poor people, that's a party."

I: "Inviting the poor, the crippled, the lame, means that they'll be able to enjoy all the country's amusements, the clubs, the health resorts, the hotels: what has happened in Cuba."

ALEJANDRO: "Before that we have to edu-

cate the poor, cure the sick, dress the badly
clothed, so they can be at a party, in a club,
and have it be a joyful party."

> *And you will be happy.*
> *For they cannot pay you,*
> *but you will have your recompense in the*
>   *resurrection of the just.*

"It seems to me that happiness is love."

"On the other hand, the prize of the rich,
the prize the system gives them, is that of
their selfishness, and it's a very sad prize, according to Jesus."

FELIPE: "He says the recompense of these
others will be in the resurrection of the just.
It seems to me that what he means is that
when the people realize that somebody who
has died has served other people, then that
man is resurrected among the people. He's
respected, and that's his recompense, it
seems to me. There's a remembrance of him,
and sorrow that he's gone and so they feel it
in the community. It seems to me that's his
recompense; I don't know if I'm mistaken."

ESPERANZA: "That's not much, that they
should just remember me."

CESAR: "It depends on what you mean by
the resurrection of the just, because that resurrection could be like in a classless society,
living in the memory of the people. Or it could
be communion with God after death. The two
things can exist together, and they are certain, once the people take power, to live in the

memory of the people, and besides to live in communion with God after death."

I: "Esperanza is right; it's not much that they should just remember you, that maybe they'd name a street after you."

FELIPE: "But there are others who stay alive in the memory of the people, but like something negative. People say: 'He's better off dead!'"

I: "What do you think about so many anonymous heroes, who have died for the people, and their heroism has never been known? Leonel Rugama, the young poet who died in the urban warfare in Managua, has stayed very much alive in the memories of many, but he had written that one had to die without expecting to be remembered 'in the press or in history.' "

DIONISIO: "He was the one who sat in the last seat and will be taken to the first seat. The best thing about Leonel Rugama was his ideals of justice, and the resurrection of the just will come on the day when the justice he died for is a reality. The life and death of Leonel Rugama will be justified because he won't have died in vain. He'll be resurrected among the people through the works of the people who'll be doing what he wanted."

I: "Dionisio has done well to notice that little word that Jesus said, the 'just.' Because he has spoken of the resurrection of the 'just' and he doesn't speak of the resurrection of everybody, including the exploiters. And we already know what the word 'just' means in

the Bible. Justice is social justice and liberation; the unjust one is the oppressor, and the
just one is the liberator. God is absolute justice; and his main attribute is that of the Just
One: The one who punishes injustice, and the
one who comes to the oppressed and listens to
the cries of the poor, and the one who liber-
ates. And the just are the ones who have
struggled for the establishment of justice on
earth. They are going to be resurrected, according to Jesus, and they are the ones who
have given the party they're talking about
here, the sharing of joy and abundance in the
world. Dionisio, although he's an atheist, has
expressed this resurrection very well, because the faith in resurrection that Marxist
atheists have is very similar to that of Christians. People have believed that there's a
great difference between Christians and
Marxists about this business of resurrection,
but it's not true. There are a great number of
songs, poems, and posters, that say that Che
is alive, and that many others are alive, all
those who have given their lives for the people. It's not just to be alive in the memory of
the people but to be alive *in* the people. Dead
as a person but personally alive with the life
of total humanity. 'HOMELAND OR DEATH, WE
SHALL OVERCOME,' it seems to me Fidel explained in a speech saying that even when
dead, if we died for the people, we shall overcome. It's like what Christ said: 'Even though
he is dead he will live.' And this is the same
communion with God that César speaks of. In

the Bible, God is love, understanding love to be social justice, and to be joined to this love is to be alive forever. Jesus has begun by saying: 'When they invite you to a wedding party.' And it's because this great party of humanity of which we've talked will celebrate a wedding party with Love. What does Esperanza say?"

ESPERANZA: "Now I agree."

I: "So now you do find hope, right?"

14.

"If You Do Not Become as Children"

(Matthew 18:1–5)

On that occasion the disciples approached Jesus and asked him:
"Who is most important in the kingdom of heaven?"

TERESITA: "From the question they asked it's clear they wanted to be very important."

ALEJANDRO: "From Jesus' answer we can see that, after all, in the kingdom some are more important than others. But the most important ones are different from the ones they thought."

LAUREANO: "Their desire to be outstanding wasn't bad. The one who's struggling for a revolution also tries to be outstanding. But you have to see what kind of importance they want to have."

Then Jesus called a child, put him in their midst, and said:

138

*"To tell you the truth, if you don't change
  and become like children,
you're not going to enter the kingdom of
  heaven."*

MARCELINO: "The first thing I see is that
the child is good and knows no malice. Maybe
because the child is only just created and is
closer to God. And to enter the kingdom, we
must get rid of all the evil that we've picked
up as we've grown up."

WILLIAM: "Evil that's mostly part of the
system and that wasn't in the child."

GLORIA: "And children too, because they're
pure, aren't oppressors, they don't exploit
anybody; instead they can be oppressed and
exploited. And I think for that reason too we
have the example of the child, because that's
the way we ought to be, without the urge
to dominate that grown-up people usually
have."

LAUREANO: "I think it's all very clear: he
gives the example of the child because children are the ones who serve. Children never
ask to be served; they're just told to serve.
And it's clear that the one that serves the
others is the most important one."

I said that in the language of Jesus, and
also in other ancient languages, they used the
same word for "servant" as for "child." Legally children were in the same situation
as slaves, and in the thinking of that time
they weren't clearly distinguished from one
another any more than they were distin-

guished in the language. And what is the practical lesson that Jesus is giving us here?

LAUREANO: "It's quite clear and simple, I think: we must serve others."

OLIVIA: "And I see that Jesus here too wants to teach us equality. Because all children consider themselves equal. Poor kids can walk with rich kids and they don't even realize they're walking with rich kids because, in their simplicity, all kids are equal to them. Then out of this we get the lesson of living all equal, in a life of simplicity and equality."

WILLIAM: "The child is a communist, as humanity was communist at the start. But the system that we've had for thousands of years makes children selfish. Teresita and I try to train our children so they won't lose their communist tendency. When Juan asks if something belongs to him, we tell him it belongs to him and to his little sister and to Elvis and to Ernesto and to Alejandro."

I said that "change in attitude" is an expression we often find in the Gospel and it used to be translated as "conversion." Here Jesus makes it clear what this change is: "if you don't change and become like children." It's to make us new people and to organize society again the way it was in the beginning and the way children are before they're corrupted by the system.

ESPERANZA: "And maybe the child that he put in their midst was an orphan child."

So then, the most important ones in the
kingdom of heaven
are the ones who humble themselves and be-
come like this child.

OSCAR: "You're screwed then if you try to get into the kingdom of heaven, man. Hell! Am I going to be letting them exploit me and not do anything? Am I going to be humiliated forever? [After a pause] I think that, like in every political movement, there are some who lead. Jesus is saying there that we mustn't expect to have a place next to him because we haven't fought yet; we're together in the same movement, but if I don't fight he can't give me any place. The disciples were thinking that they'd pick that up free for nothing."

"But the struggle in this movement is to serve others and not to dominate."

OSCAR: "I'm talking in the sense of a real revolution, where nobody ever thinks of getting ahead of anybody, only of serving everybody."

FELIPE: "I think too that we can say to Oscar that being humiliated is one thing and humbling yourself is another. If I humble myself through my own free will, that's very different."

OLIVIA: "And it can happen too that you don't want to be humiliated, and you prefer to be with the ones who humiliate the masses; or else you identify with the masses, who are being forcibly humiliated."

OSCAR: "There it teaches that you ought to humble yourself and it's good. But it doesn't mean you ought to let yourself get squashed, and that's it, that's the end! It seems to me there's no point in that. And Jesus isn't teaching us that."

WILLIAM: "This humbling yourself that Christ talks about is the renunciation of selfishness, and only through this renunciation can we free ourselves from all oppression."

I: "In those times there were political movements that could seem revolutionary, but they really weren't, because their objective wasn't the conquest of power by the people but the domination of one class over the others and of Israel over the other peoples. And when Jesus was talking of a new kingdom, the disciples understood him with this same mentality. That's why they've asked Jesus who is going to be the most 'important,' expecting that they'll all be in important jobs. And what Jesus does is something very revolutionary: to put a child in front of them and say that's the most important one. It's almost as if he'd put a slave in front of them."

And he who receives in my name a child like this one, receives me.

LAUREANO: "And that's even more radical, because he identifies himself with the defenseless one, with the weak one. He says we must see his person in the oppressed one."

FELIPE: "In other words, anybody who

struggles for a child struggles for the cause of Jesus Christ too. And that's what the revolutionaries do who struggle so there'll be day nurseries, maternity rooms, kindergartens, schools. And they struggle not just for the children but for all the unprotected."

A lady: "Here's an example right in our community: we keep our children out of school so they can work for us, and that's exploiting children, and that's like exploiting Christ himself."

FELIPE: "But above all the child has to be taught all we're reading here, what's said here about the kingdom of heaven and about the children, the little ones. And this is more important than what they teach in school, because there are people that know a lot, but everything they know they use to screw the humble ones, the little ones."

(Against the church door there's a noisy bang from a stone that little John, the son of William and Teresita, has thrown with his sling.)

15.

The "Scandal"

(Matthew 18:6–9)

*Anyone who makes any of these little ones
   who believe in me stumble,
it would be better for that person to be
   thrown into the sea
with a millstone around his neck.*

I said that last Sunday we heard the passage where Jesus talks about children, and we realized that by "children" Jesus meant all the weak and oppressed too. Here he clearly refers to the oppressed when he shifts from "children" to "little ones." Here also there is a word that has traditionally been badly translated as "scandal," when it means an obstacle placed on your path to make you fall, what in Latin is called *scandalum*, and this is not what we mean now by "scandalize." Jesus isn't talking about people who make other people fall into sin; he's just talking about people who make the little ones stumble.

EDUARDO: "And the little ones aren't only kids. They can be grown people."

OLIVIA: "Even though Jesus was maybe thinking especially about children or because he saw that child there is why he began to talk about oppression; because when there's injustice children are the first to suffer, and it's seeing children suffer that makes us suffer so much, their parents and their older brothers and sisters. And the capitalists are the ones that are an obstacle so children can't grow up and develop like men and women. And those children, if they get to grow up, it's only to have other children just as oppressed."

ALEJANDRO: "I think the person who's an obstacle to the child (a stumbling block, right?) is the one who brings him up badly, so as to make him a slave of the system, destroying his personality. And they do this with all the little ones, not just with the children of the poor but with the children of the rich too. And those are the people Jesus says we have to get rid of, maybe not in such a hard way as he says, throwing them into the water, but we'll have to get rid of them some way."

OSCAR: "Alejandro, the rich are always making poor people stumble, making them sin, because they stuff them with the ideas of the system and they make them accept all the injustices. And they're a stumbling block for the people, because they prevent the people from making progress."

Woe to the people who create the obstacles!
Obstacles are necessary,
but God help the one who's the cause of them!

WILLIAM: "There always have to be obstacles to the advancement of humanity; it's a historical necessity, because every evolution is made by overcoming obstacles. There are obstacles that are natural ones and there are other obstacles set up by people themselves; and Christ says God help the person who's an obstacle to human advancement."

ESPERANZA: "He says God help him because every obstacle to human advancement has to be eliminated."

And if your hand or your foot is acting like an obstacle to you,
cut it off and throw it away;
because it's better for you to go through life with a hand missing or a foot missing
than to be cast into eternal fire with your two hands and your two feet.
And if your eye is acting like an obstacle to you,
tear it out and throw it away;
because it's better to go through life with just one eye
than to be cast with your two eyes into hell's fire.

LAUREANO: "I think that can mean your family, or any other relatives you may have.

He says you have to be extreme; if anything's an obstacle, you have to cut it off."

ALEJANDRO: "And not just your family; anything closer to you, on your person, if it's an obstacle, you have to cut if off; you have to be extreme in that too."

PANCHO: "These words of Christ can be used too by an evil government that wants to get rid of people that are obstacles to it."

OSCAR: "And they *do* do it. But Christ isn't talking about them; he's talking about us. We ought to cut off anything that keeps us from entering the kingdom, even though the thing is something that's a part of our own person. And a while back he talked about what we've got to do with the ones who are oppressing the little people. Whoever's getting in the way can't be saved: into the water with them!"

"The 'hell's fire' mentioned here," I said, "in Hebrew is literally 'Gehenna's fire.' Gehenna was the dump heap of Jerusalem, where the trash was burned, and according to Isaiah the bodies of Israel's enemies were thrown there too."

Do not scorn any of these little ones.
For I tell you that in heaven
their angels are always in the presence of
*   my heavenly Father.*

I said that in Hebrew "angel" has the concrete meaning of messenger. Some have interpreted Jesus as speaking of the children's 'guardian angels,' but what he's saying is simply that God is always receiving the children's messengers (as the ambassadors of a powerful nation are received at court).

OLIVIA: "The ones fighting in the mountains, maybe those are the ambassadors, the angels, the ones that are defending the oppressed."

I: "The messengers of the little ones are in direct contact with God. That's what Christ says. And that's very beautiful, that phrase of his."

FELIPE: "It always seems that the weak have nobody to defend them. The people, the *campesinos*, let's say, it seems we're abandoned. But there are always people struggling for our freedom, even some upper-class people, and that's how come there were those angels."

OSCAR: "I was just thinking that in a community there's always a leader, and that leader is a kind of messenger to God, and God sends his message to the community through that leader. And that leader can be William, Ernesto, Laureano, or anybody."

"Or you," I said to Oscar.

OSCAR: "Or me; anybody that can make the community see what's good and what's evil; those people are like ambassadors to God carrying the message from the community to God and from God to the community."

JUAN BOSCO: "And Che Guevara could be an angel?"

OLIVIA: "He, and everybody like him who has died, and all the ones they're killing right now, they're like envoys from the poor to God; they put us in contact with God, that's what Christ is saying."

PANCHO: "Then we really ought to feel proud, us little people, because we're greater than any of those bastards."

I: "That's what Christ is talking about here, about the greatness that little people have."

FELIPE: "I think he has said that the bosses ought to be like children, very humble people, like representatives of the people, simple people, very good people. And all the people ought to be like them too, humble, simple, just, and that way they'll be in close contact with God. And anybody that's screwing those humble people, we'll have to find a way to get rid of them."

I asked if anybody had anything to add.

"Nothing more."

16.

The Brother's Pardon

(Matthew 18:15–22)

*If your brother has sinned, scold him all
    alone.*
*If he heeds you, you have gained your
    brother.*

ELVIS: "Very good advice, that. Because if
you see someone doing something bad and
you let it pass, and say, 'What's it to me?' that
person doesn't reform. But if you make him
see that he's done wrong, maybe he can reform. That's what it means there about he
has gained his brother."

ALEJO: "Another possibility is for you to accuse your brother before the policeman or before the judge. And Jesus says no, that you
should go and talk with him in private and
make him see that he's done wrong, and that
way maybe you can gain him."

TOMAS: "He says that, it seems to me, so
that we can live under better conditions. And
let's not live the way we sometimes live, that

if someone does something bad, the others don't correct him but just concentrate on talking against the comrade, right?"

PANCHO: "This is probably for a community in which everybody is very aware. But if somebody like us goes to somebody to try to correct him, that person would say: 'Man, don't be silly, don't be giving me advice when you're doing worse things.' "

FELIPE: "In a Managua parish where there's a mixture of exploiters, rich people, bandits, maybe even murderers, this doesn't work. There people can't correct each other. But Jesus is talking to the community of his disciples, a community like this one, in which, just the same, we're not all perfect; we can have faults."

LAUREANO: "But the truth is that we do very few evil things."

But if he doesn't heed you, then call one or two more,
so that any accusation can be based on the word of two or three witnesses.

TOMAS: "It seems to me he says that because the other person is maybe already angry. That's why he must bring two more witnesses, so they can see he's not angry with the other one. He only wants to reform him, and he wants harmony. If not, tomorrow or some other day the other one can get even sorer and they could even kill each other, see? And then you have even more troubles."

ALEJANDRO: "It seems to me that stuff about the witnesses is because three of them are like a small community court."

If he doesn't heed them then tell the congregation;
and if he doesn't heed the congregation,
then he must be considered a pagan or a tax collector.

I: "The publicans or tax collectors were the ones who collaborated with the Roman occupation, and the religious Jews considered them excluded from the Jewish community just like the pagans. But here Jesus isn't concerned with religious questions. He's saying that if somebody does evil and doesn't reform he ought to be excommunicated from the community. The unjust person (and not the person of another religion), that's the one that ought to be considered by us as 'pagan' or 'publican.'"

ALEJANDRO: "Which is like saying the oppressor or the collaborator of the oppressor."

"He has removed himself from the community. Suppose one day there's a community effort on all the islands to grow wheat, to grow rice, to grow fruit. There's one guy that acts selfishly and works only for himself. He has removed himself from the community. He's outside, but we have to fight to get him back in."

FELIPE: "For Christ the ones who don't believe in God are the ones who don't love their neighbor, the ones who don't want to live in harmony with their companions."

TOMAS: "Those you've got to throw out, of course. They would break the unity. They'd be like ghosts."

We all laughed. He continued: "What we have to watch out for is so that somebody doesn't go on being a nuisance. That's why you say: 'See, I'm going to church to straighten this out'; it's not because they're going to beat you there or do you any harm. But to go to San Carlos and look for the cops, that's what pagans do."

I: "If the community is united there's no need to carry the quarrel outside, right? What Christ says is very interesting: You mustn't accuse anyone to the police judge in San Carlos. It's the community that must judge."

TOMAS: "Yes, we're together here, and here we can solve our problems."

OSCAR: "I think it's better for them to set the cops on you, instead of the whole town, the community, shouting 'whore' at me. I'd feel like shit then; I'd rather have a cop take me to jail."

PANCHO: "I feel like Oscar: if one of us commits a robbery right here and right away they show him up and we all see his face, well, it would be terrible. It's better for a cop to take you to jail and you pay a fine. That wouldn't be so shameful because the cop is a worse robber."

I: "In Cuba it's the people that judge lawsuits and differences within a town, and they do this with admirable wisdom, by means of what they call 'Popular Tribunals.' "

MYRIAM: "It's clear they're doing what the Bible says."

FELIPE: "And if our Nicaraguan society changed and became like Christ wants, we wouldn't have an authority and an army that exist only to screw the poor and not to defend them. We'd keep united on a basis of understanding and dialogue and not on a basis of screwing each other, throwing each other in jail or punching each other, like now when we have the cops."

> *I tell you the truth:*
> *what you tie in this world will be tied also in*
> *heaven,*
> *and what you untie in this world will be un-*
> *tied in heaven.*

I: "This means that everything the community decides will be ratified by God. In the Gospel according to Saint Matthew the word 'heaven' means God (because of the Jewish custom of not mentioning God). This is the same power that Jesus formerly gave to Peter, and now he says the whole community has it."

ALEJANDRO: "So the verdict of the people can't be appealed."

OSCAR: "Look, Ernesto, if the community doesn't pardon me, and I beg God's pardon directly, wouldn't there be a possibility of being pardoned?"

ALEJANDRO: "And who has he offended? A brother, right? Well, why should he go and beg the pardon of somebody else who isn't the one he's offended?"

ELVIS: "I don't think there are two justices, one of the community and another of God. If you don't beg pardon of the community, what other pardon can you get, if the community is Christ himself? It seems to me that guy is screwed."

> *I also tell you that if two of you here on earth*
> *   agree to ask for something in prayer,*
> *my Father who is in heaven will grant it to*
> *   you.*
> *Because wherever two or three are gathered*
> *   in my name,*
> *there am I in the midst of them.*

TOMAS: "The agreeing that's talked about here, it seems to me that it's this way: all of us here are in agreement, God's also in agreement with us. I say to Manuel, for example, or some other guy, or anybody: 'Man, let's come to an agreement to do something.' Right? Then that one gets somebody else and now there's three of us. Then I think the thing gets going, that God comes to an agreement with you, because the three people are in agreement. You could almost say they're like the three Divine Persons. And the three Divine Persons are like a single true God. And the three persons who are in agreement would be three who are united with God."

FELIPE: "It seems to me that being united in the name of God is loving each other. There are others who are united, but not through love."

WILLIAM: "For example, in a capitalistic company, or in an army of repression."

ALEJANDRO: "Those people are together, but they're not united. They've become bastards. That's not what we call unity!"

OSCAR: "And people that come together in a church to celebrate communion aren't either, all mixed together rich and poor."

OLIVIA: "Those people are just looking for individual salvation for each one, and not unity. Or they go to ask God for money or think only of themselves. Money's very important; without money you can't live, but it ought to be divided up."

LAUREANO: "But you can too live without money, Doña Olivia. In a perfect society there won't be any need for money. Then everybody'll have everything they need to live. There'll be loads of beans; there'll be loads of sugar and all that stuff, clothes, and, you know, all the rest."

WILLIAM: "Yes, I believe if we ask God as individuals, God's not going to make a miracle for us; but if we unite to ask God for something, we're going to get it, through ourselves, through our unity; because if we're agreed about asking we'll also be agreed about acting. And that unity is Christ himself; he's the community, he's the people."

FELIPE: "And from that community they've already expelled the one who was evil, the unjust one."

OSCAR: "And if unfortunately that guy that they expelled like that is innocent?"

I: "The people's verdict is the verdict of God, says Christ. According to Christ the people make no mistakes; what the people say will be approved in heaven."

FELIPE: "It seems like magic, but I think he says that because when two or three are together it's because there's understanding and love between them. If there's love, Christ is among them; he is love among them. And then they can do everything, because love is what's going to change the world."

WILLIAM: "And this has been said before but it's worth repeating: Cuba is now a community united by the love that people have for each other. And Christ is there with them even though they don't realize it. And there what the Gospel says is fulfilled, that when people unite to help each other and love each other, they get everything they want, and that's why the revolution has made all those miracles there."

ADAN: "And there, if somebody's screwing the community, they get rid of that person."

"The Gospel says it very clearly, but if in society there's no love, we pick up the book and read, and we get all confused; we get confused because we don't have love, to fulfill the Gospel we must be like the Cubans."

WILLIAM: "Whether or not they believe Christ is in their midst is secondary, it seems to me. There are Christians who are very aware of Christ and it does them no good, because if they're not united to the other people, Christ isn't with them. It's the kind of Christianity that's broadcast on that program 'The Voice of Hope.' "

OSCAR: "And I imagine Christ isn't concerned about his name. Why should he want us to be saying and saying his name and not love each other? On the other hand, there's others who don't believe in him and who love each other. Well, that's what he wants, for them to love each other."

I said that in the language of the Bible "name" doesn't mean the name of a person but the person himself, or also what we now call the character or the spirit of a person. When Christ speaks of gathering in his name he doesn't mean that they're going to be mentioning his name but that they'll be gathered in his spirit, in agreement with his teachings and his message. That community will have such great power because he will be in the midst of them.

> *Then Peter went and asked Jesus:*
> *"Lord, how many times, if my brother does*
>   *me evil, do I have to forgive him?*
> *As many as seven times?"*
> *Jesus answered him:*
> *"I do not say as many as seven times,*
> *but as many as seventy times seven."*

FELIPE: "That's sure tough, right?"

I: "It's tough for the one who forgives but for the other one it's nice."

LAUREANO: "Well, hell, are you going to let them screw you? It's unfair for them to be screwing you."

ALEJANDRO: "That's what the community's for, to correct that individual, to run him out if necessary. Because, according to the Gospel, this is about a 'brother,' another member of the community."

I: "There are people who offend you, of course. The question is whether you're going to forgive them or going to go on hating them."

OLIVIA: "Well, if we have hatred and bitterness, that's the end of the community."

LAUREANO: "But if I'm in a community and I know they're going to pardon me every time I shit on them, I'll go on shitting on them forever. That's why I think you shouldn't forgive any bully."

OSCAR: "Look: if I offend somebody and I beg his pardon and he forgives me, it seems to me that I'm ashamed of what I've done; I'm not going to do it again. There he says seventy times seven, but he knows what he's saying. Why did he say it? Because if he does it once, he's not going to do it twice, because we're in a community of conscience."

LAUREANO: "The first thing we have to do is to have that community."

I: "We're beginning to have it. Jesus tells us how that community must be organized, how to be united, and how to forgive each other."

OSCAR: "It would be good to be discussing this every Sunday, to understand it better and to be more aware."

17.

The Servant Who Wouldn't Forgive

(Matthew 18:23–35)

This is the parable of the servant who owed ten talents (many millions) to a king, and the king was going to sell him with all his family, but later he took pity on him and forgave him the debt. The man later throttled another servant because he owed him a small amount, and he put him in jail until he paid the whole debt.

> *Then the Lord sent for him and said to him:*
> *"Evil servant! I forgave you all that debt of*
>   *yours, because you begged me to.*
> *You too should have taken pity on your*
>   *companion as I took pity on you."*
> *And the Lord was so angered that he ordered*
>   *him punished until he paid the whole*
>   *debt.*
> *And Jesus ended by saying:*

161

"*So also my heavenly Father will do with
     you
if each one does not forgive his brother in
     his heart.*"

"We will be evil too if we ask God's pardon
without pardoning our neighbor."

"Then we don't even have the right to ask
for pardon."

"But if you forgive your neighbor, then you
do have a right to be forgiven."

"But I believe one thing: any who ask forgiveness of their neighbor, it's like asking
God's forgiveness. It's really not God that
forgives directly; it's our neighbor who forgives us some evil that we've done. That's
why we must seek our comrade's forgiveness
instead of saying to God: 'God forgive me.' "

I: "It seems too that this parable is telling
us that the love that people have for each
other is the very love of God for us."

MANUEL: "I believe that only when there is
love can you forgive. If there's bitterness and
there's no love, then there's no forgiveness.
The forgiveness has to be real: you have to
forget what they've done to you."

NATALIA: "Yes, because if you're not going
to forgive from the heart, you shouldn't say
you forgave somebody because then you'd be
lying. If you really forgave, you forgot it. But
if you just *say*, 'I forgave,' that's nothing."

"Notice that Jesus specifies that detail:
that the forgiveness has to come 'from the
heart.' "

LAUREANO: "This Gospel is silly!"

Several people: "Why is it silly?"

LAUREANO: "Several people have talked, but nobody has said anything good. And I haven't found anything good to say either. All you've talked about is forgiveness and forgiveness. I don't see anything in this Gospel against injustice."

ARMANDO: "This Gospel isn't like you say. It also talks against injustice. Because the person that wouldn't forgive, the one that owed the millions, he was really committing an injustice: he wanted to strangle another person for a few pesos that he owed him."

JULIO: "I think this Gospel is revolutionary, because it deals with the poor and the rich. And I see here a lesson for the rich, because the first to be pardoned was rich, and the second, who couldn't pay such a tiny amount, was poor. The Lord puts rich and poor on an equal plane. He says that just as the rich guy was forgiven, the poor guy must be forgiven too. But it happens that in this society the rich are forgiven for the evil things they do but the poor are shoved into jail because they are poor. In this example Jesus is showing us the poor and the rich as equals. The millionaire was forgiven through charity, through love, and just as he was forgiven he should also forgive the other weaker person and have for him also charity, love. And we can give an example using the words of today: at present we see that the rich have no compassion for the poor. If the rich had love for the poor, and the poor for the rich, that would mean there wouldn't be rich or poor any more: that's love! So let everybody live equal. And then we wouldn't have that stuff about selling the poor man with all his family to pay what he owes. And God can't forgive their sins, then, until they stop exploiting."

DOÑA JUSTA: "The one who had many millions was loaded down with sins."

ARMANDO: "And who has said that forgiveness isn't revolutionary? Because the first thing you have to forgive are the economic debts. If not, you don't have that forgiveness from the heart that Christ talks about. Because if somebody is economically strangling his neighbor, how can he say that in his heart he has nothing against him? And so God is going to treat him like he treats his laborers, the ones who depend on him, the ones he exploits."

MARCELINO: "The poor aren't the ones who must have compassion for the rich, who are strangling them; they ought to be struggling against the injustices of the rich. It's the rich who ought to take pity on the poor and stop strangling them. But when the poor are in power it will be up to the poor to have pity on the rich, because otherwise we fall into the same thing as they do; we'll become like them."

JULIO: "It's not that those who are poor now are going to be in the place of the rich, and then we'll say: 'Now they are the poor ones, we'll get them because now we can.' I believe that's not the question; it's about being equal."

CESAR: "Of course this Gospel talks about forgiveness, but I believe too that forgiveness is revolutionary. It's not necessary for the Gospel to be talking only against the rich for it to be revolutionary. Because the revolution is inside you too. As long as you haven't revolutionized yourself, you can't be a real revolutionary. If you're a revolutionary that doesn't forgive, you're not a just revolutionary, and then you're not going to be able to make a good revolution. And this Gospel today teaches us to be revolutionaries before we begin to make a revolution. You're going to make the revolution when you've been revolutionary enough, that is, when you've revolutionized yourself."

FELIPE: "The one who owed those millions was rich, because a nobody doesn't owe that much money. It seems to me that Jesus gives the example of a rich person because he wants to give the example of an exploiter. Everything the rich have got they've stolen from us, because all their riches have been got with our labor; and now all their injustices are forgiven them, but they don't forgive us; they throw us into jail when we owe them a bit. Someday, it seems to me, God will settle accounts with them through the people and he'll collect the whole debt. But at the end Jesus says we all must also forgive our neighbors in our hearts. Who knows if we have that capacity to forgive each other, or if we're like that rich person, like that exploiter."

BOSCO: "At the beginning he said that the kingdom of heaven *is* like a king who forgives a debt. And he tells the whole story. He means that in that society of perfect communism, we're all going to forgive everything, and anyone who doesn't forgive is going to be treated like an exploiter, like a reactionary."

ELVIS: "Yes, because we already know that the kingdom of heaven on earth will be a kingdom of love, without hatred, without bitterness, without the divisions that humanity now has."

JULIO: "I believe this too will come when there's equality and nobody owes nobody."

ALEJANDRO: "But let's move to the practical and not stick just on theory. Because here among us I see defects. Let's not concentrate just on seeing evil in exploiters. We need to practice these things a lot. Hatred, bitterness, injustice can happen and do happen in our community, among neighbors, among people in the same family, among couples, among friends. And so we too must learn in our community this practical lesson for forgiveness. We the poor must forgive each other, too. If we don't, we're not good comrades, good revolutionaries."

18.

Jesus Talks about Marriage

(Matthew 19:1–12)

Then some Pharisees approached Jesus to
make him fall into a trap,
and they asked him:
"Is it permitted to divorce one's wife for any
reason?"

MANUEL: "It was a trap, because if he said
yes, they were going to say he was against
marriage and if he said no, they were going to
say he was against the law of Moses, which
allowed divorce."

SILVESTRE: "But they supposed he wouldn't
want to say a man could leave a woman for any
reason."

CARLOS (a Spanish priest who had just married and who had come to Solentiname with
his wife, Concha): "The Pharisees knew that
Jesus was in favor of freedom and at the same
time in favor of love, and with this question
they wanted to put him up against the wall."

167

MANUEL: "Like when they asked him about the woman taken in adultery; he either was for adultery or he was for cruelty."

I: "The law of Deuteronomy said the man could abandon the woman when he was not pleased with her, and all he had to do was sign a document giving up the wife. But it didn't say the wife could leave the husband. And the Pharisees foresee that Jesus is not going to accept that injustice, and that he'll set himself up against the law, which was a law of the Bible, given by God to Moses."

He answered them:
"Have you not read in the Scriptures
that he who made them in the beginning
'made them man and wife'?
He also said:
'For this reason man will leave his father
and his mother to unite with his wife
and the two shall be a single one.'
So that they are not two now but only one.
So that what God has joined together
let man not split it apart."

GOYITO: "Then he means that the law of Moses was getting a little away from the law of God. It must be that law belonged more to human beings than to God."

MARCELINO: "God created people in his image, which means he created them to be a union of people like God is, and he created them with two sexes so they could unite and be like a single God."

REBECA: "It's love that unites them, but

since God is love, he says that God has united them."

CARLOS: "And what love has united, people can't separate. In this case it's the law of Moses."

I: "It also means that God created the two sexes equal, because he created the human race free, without any kind of exploitation. The loss of Paradise was the beginning of exploitation. That's why God announced to the woman that from then on she would be dominated by man. Just as he announced the future sorrows of humanity (to give birth in sorrow), exploitation in work, conflict with nature, death. But here Christ is making it clear that if exploitation wasn't with us from the beginning, there's no reason why it has to be with us forever, and that we are called to reconquer the equality and the liberty of Paradise."

GOYO: "So he *was* departing a bit from the law."

Then they asked him:
"Why, then, did Moses order them to give the woman a divorce certificate,
and thus to abandon her?"
Jesus said to them:
"Precisely through the harshness of your hearts
Moses allowed you to divorce your wives.
But it was not so at the beginning."

ALEJANDRO: "Moses had given them that law because it was practical."

I: "It was practical, in those times when woman had no rights. She was simply man's property, like a thing, or like a slave, and that's why Jesus says it was because of their 'harshness.' You couldn't do any more in the social system of that time, and Moses ordered that at least the man should sign a document when he rejected his wife, declaring her free."

ALEJANDRO: "It was a slightly liberating law, and therefore it was a law also given by God. But it wasn't a totally liberating law, and later there could be a better law. It was the most that people could accept in that regime of slavery."

I: "The same thing happened with slavery: God had forbidden the Israelites to have slaves, because he had freed them all from the slavery of Egypt. But as they didn't obey, through 'the harshness of their hearts' (through the historical conditions of that time), in Leviticus there are also laws that regulated slavery and softened it, ordering that each jubilee year all slaves should be freed."

FELIPE: "The Pharisees thought everything ought to stay the same, that what was in Moses' time ought to be forever. And they believed every law was sacred. Jesus made them see that the marriage law they had was given to them by their selfishness, like the law of slavery and the law of private property."

ELVIS: "I think paradise is really going to be the society of the future when people have no selfishness. It's clear that if Jesus talks about

how people were in paradise it's to say that
people are going to get to be like that; otherwise it wouldn't make sense to say how they
had been in paradise."

CARLOS: "I think the law has a temporary
character. It's been useful to people, because
there was a lot of injustice. But the law has
slowly changed, and a moment will come when
people won't need any law. Christ really came
to suppress all laws except the law of love.
Saint Paul also used to say: 'Down with the
law!' But it's hard for us; we cling to the law,
because we're still deep in sin."

> *I say to you that he who dismisses his wife,*
> *except in the case of infidelity,*
> *and marries another woman, commits adul-*
> *tery,*
> *and he who marries the divorced woman also*
> *commits adultery.*

FELIPE: "Well, I'd say it was a mistake to
leave a wife because another woman is more
likable or prettier or for any reason. But at the
present time the word 'adultery,' it seems to
me, no longer has much meaning. Let's say it's
an injustice."

GOYO: "It's a bad mixture: like when you
have a pure thing, a liquid for example, and
you add something else, and it comes out all
weak; it isn't what it was any more. It's a falsification. That's to adulterate."

I: "It's a falsification, as Goyo said, like is
done with milk and many other products, and

therefore it's an injustice. It's falsifying love, adulterating it."

GLORIA: "It says the man can leave the woman in case of infidelity. And the woman, in that case, can she throw the man out?"

LAUREANO: "Women are always getting deceived! "

GLORIA: "That's *machismo*."

GOYO: "In those times there was a law that just protected men. And Christ places man equal with woman, but not through another law, through love, which is greater than the law, and harder."

ALEJANDRO: "So he's on the side of the women because he's on the side of the weak."

I: "He's against the law, which oppresses the weak. Just as the other time, in a case of adultery, he took the part of the woman and against the law. Jesus opposed the divorce law because it was a law that oppressed women. But if prohibition of divorce is changed into a law oppressive for some men or for some women, it seems to me that Jesus wasn't going to be in agreement with this new law."

CARLOS: "I think that above this new divorce law Jesus is putting something else, which is love. If love really doesn't exist any more, then there's nothing. What difference does it make if there is or isn't a law! Are we going to say that divorce is good? No. We are going to defend love. But if the union is broken, you've already sinned, now there's nothing to be done. And it's not only a case of infidelity. Maybe some are sexually very pure, and they don't love anymore, and then the union is broken too."

OLIVIA: "What's important is for the two people to be a single thing. If it's not like that, then they have no reason to be united by any law."

CARLOS: "But out of this we get that marriage ought to be forever. Because love, what God has united, ought to be forever. And this can apply also to friendship, which ought to be forever."

GUSTAVO (a young South American who was expelled from Cuba for something to do with his private life): "I believe, like Carlos says, that this can apply to friendship, but it can also apply to another kind of relations that are misunderstood by most people, and in which there can also be true love. At present, in many countries, among advanced groups and even more among frankly revolutionary groups, we're beginning to understand that the homosexuals have also been oppressed. And we're also beginning now to see their liberation as human beings. I believe this liberation can come only through the revolution, in socialism. It's a pity that the revolutions of the past haven't understood it this way. The Cuban Revolution, for example, that has changed so many things and has opened so many new paths to all us Latin Americans, hasn't understood this problem clearly. I believe it's a subject that ought to be placed before Christian revolutionaries, and Marxist revolutionaries, and that's why I've brought it up here."

GOYO: "According to Christ, in a union, of love or friendship, God is the one who unites. The ones who separate, if there's a separation, are human beings. Separation comes because they have adulterated, falsified love, or they've been unfaithful; they have falsified faith."

CARLOS: "The moment you don't love your wife, even though you live with her, you've already separated. Some couples may stay together, because of the law or some other outside reasons, but the only union is love. And love is always free. Maybe the church insists on non-separation so the union won't break up so easily. That seems to me a little trivial, stupid. But at any rate you can't separate calmly, because love has been smashed and that's terrible."

I: "We can sum all this up by saying that what God (love) has united cannot be separated by people, by any human law. But what God (love) does not unite, cannot be united by people, by any human law."

GOYO: "If one person is united with another, they're a single one. Let's say that I own a thing half-and-half with someone else; I can't get rid of it, sell it, because the other guy has his part also, and he can't get rid of it because both of us own it. A single thing. That's the love that God has given us."

FELIPE: "Neither the man nor the woman

can get rid of each other. They'll be on an equal
plane, as they were created at the beginning,
man and woman, companion and companion,
not master and slave. And it will be free love,
without oppression, and society will be free."

I: "And Jesus, when he talks about the love
of the human couple, doesn't pay attention to
the law of Moses or any other law. What he
mentions is paradise. I think he's telling us
that love and paradise are the same thing.
And also that our goal is paradise."

> *His disciples then said to him:*
> *"If this is the case of the man in relation to*
> *his wife,*
> *it's better not to marry."*
> *Jesus said to them:*
> *"Not all can understand this,*
> *only those to whom God has given to under-*
> *stand it."*

FELIPE: "The ones who said that were men,
and their position was a very *macho* position.
As they were losing their privileges, they said
it was better to be free, because it wasn't going
to be like it was before."

I: "And Jesus tells them that in fact it's better to be free, but not for those human reasons
but for other reasons that only God lets them
understand."

CARLOS: "He gives them love to understand;
it's understood by people God gives himself to,
and God himself is love."

ANTENOR: "The disciples understood it

later, because they didn't marry; they remained celibates, that is, free, like Christ."

GOYO: "This is an even freer love."

There are men who are born eunuchs,
there are others who are made eunuchs by
    men,
and there are others who make themselves
    eunuchs
for love of the kingdom of heaven.
Let whoever can understand this under-
    stand it.

ALEJANDRO: "There are some that are physically castrated and there are others that are psychically castrated, like the case of many priests who have been left that way by religious imposition, and those are frustrated; those also have been made eunuchs by men."

CARLOS: "I agree with Alejandro, that some are castrated by a law that imposes celibacy on the priesthood, and those two things don't necessarily have to go together. It's a quite different case when a priest has the charisma of the celibate."

I: "That's the case of those that Christ says castrate themselves, renounce sexual love, for love of the kingdom of God. Saint Paul found that celibacy was preferable so as to be freer to work for the kingdom. This is also the case of many revolutionaries, even non-Christians, who also have had to give up marriage for that cause. Che has said that revolutionaries in the vanguard must have a love for the people that is 'unique, indivisible,' and that therefore they must deprive themselves of the 'little dose of daily affection' enjoyed by the common person. This reminds me of a remark of Fidel, when I was talking with him in Cuba: that Che had been 'like a priest,' through his devotion and his spirit of sacrifice. He also told me on that occasion: 'Look: all the qualities of a priest are the qualities needed to make a good revolutionary.' I think that one of the main qualities he was thinking of was celibacy. And Fidel himself is one who is now married only to the revolution."

ALEJANDRO: "One who leaves his home, his wife, and his children for that cause has not been separated from love. He is separated through love to unite with them and with everyone in a greater love, what Christ calls the love of the kingdom of heaven."

GOYO: "The one who's getting married is happy because he's going to be married; and the one who doesn't get married, because of that cause, is also happy because the cause is also another love, the love of the kingdom of God."

I: "That's what Christ is saying. And he finally says: 'Those who can understand this, let them understand it.' To be able to understand this means to be capable of this devotion. Christ makes it clear that this is not for everyone. Saint Paul also considers that celibacy is better, but it is a gift for the few. And Che stresses that it's for revolutionaries in the vanguard. We Christians also know another thing: that giving up one marriage is for the sake of contracting another marriage, marriage with God (who is love). Christ here speaks of not marrying out of 'love for the kingdom of heaven.' And elsewhere he says that the kingdom of heaven is a wedding."

19.

The Workers in the Vineyard

(Matthew 20:1–16)

The owner of a vineyard made a contract with some workers in the morning for a denarius. Then he went out at different hours of the day to hire more workers telling them that he would pay them whatever was fair. At the end of the day he paid each of them a denarius. Those who started working first were angry.

> *But the owner answered one of them:*
> *"My friend, I am doing you no injustice.*
> *Did you not agree to work for a denarius?*
> *Take your pay and go away.*
> *I want to give the last worker as much as you.*
> *Don't I have the right to do what I want with*
>   *my money?*
> *Or are you annoyed because I am generous?"*

I: "You who work in the fields, let's see what you think of this parable."

"It seems to me that boss was unfair when he paid them all the same. It's true that he

179

didn't break his agreement. But if he paid, let's say, ten pesos to the ones who didn't work much, he ought to have given extra to the ones who did more work."

"If it was a question of money it would be an injustice, because all the wages he was giving were unfair. He was robbing all of them, because he should have given them the profits, not just the wages. He says he has the right to do what he wants with his money, and that's false, because that money didn't belong to him, it belonged to the workers. But what we're discussing here isn't workers and bosses but the kingdom of God. The vineyard is love. And Jesus says that, with respect to love, the same thing happens as with a boss who pays equally. That love, God isn't stealing it from anybody, while you could say that the vineyard was stolen. In love it doesn't matter what hour you begin to work, or who produces most, so to speak."

OSCAR: "I don't think the boss was unfair, because he didn't care about the work, or the profits it would bring. What he wanted was for everybody to be working. The ones who began at six earned what was coming to them; the one who began at two worked only one hour, if they stopped at three, but that had nothing to do with those who started at six. The ones who worked more were angry, of course. I can understand them, but they had no right to complain. The boss wanted to get them all together so that none would be idle."

MANUEL: "It wasn't unjust. Because, hell,

it's like if a boss says to me: 'Come and work,' and afterwards he sees Felipe and he says to him: 'You come, too,' and Felipe says: 'No, it's too late and I'm going to be earning very little.' And he says to him: 'No, man, why, I'm going to pay you well.' And he goes. He's not taking anything from me, it's a favor that he's doing him."

OLIVIA: "What I see is that the opposite happens there from what happens in real life: that the one that works most earns most. It seems that in that parable Jesus is telling us that in the new society everybody's going to get the same amount."

WILLIAM: "Not according to the work but according to the need."

FELIPE: "Here he's saying that the kingdom of heaven is like a great farm, but a farm on which everybody earns the same so nobody will feel he's more than anybody else; people aren't separated by wages."

BOSCO: "And it seems to me that when you make a revolution, the first ones that work in it shouldn't demand more than the others who join it at the end. Because the revolution is equality. It makes everybody the same."

ESPERANZA, his wife: "And that also means that it's never too late to work in the revolution, right?"

LAUREANO: "Then nobody'll get paid for what they know or what they do, except according to their needs. And everybody has almost the same needs; they have to earn the same."

I: "In the vineyard they've been working for some time, and Jesus tells this parable to the Jews, the ones who went to work first. With Israel began the history of the liberation of humanity. And the Jews believed they were going to have very special privileges in this kingdom. The fathers of the church have said the Christians were the workers that came afterwards and they were going to receive an equal reward; but Jesus speaks of different hours, and we may believe he also refers to others who came later, at the end, the atheists. There's no difference among the ones who enter at various epochs of history to work for the kingdom. Even though the first ones, says Jesus, are going to be unhappy."

FELIPE: "I see too, Ernesto, that the first ones were promised a denarius. The others were told only that they were going to get a fair wage. So they went to work without expecting the denarius, without knowing if it would be fifty cents (half a denarius) or whatever. So the ones who began to work first for the kingdom, those Jews, were holding to the religious promises that God had given them. There are others who've come later to work without thinking of those promises, thinking they're going to be given just what's fair. But in the end they're all going to receive the same reward of eternal life. But it seems that the first ones complain if these other ones receive the same reward."

> *So, then, the last shall be first,*
> *and the first shall be last.*

OLIVIA: "There's a pride among religious people, who think they're the ones that are going to transform the world, the ones that are going to bring to earth this kingdom of heaven; and the Marxists, who don't believe in God, work harder for this kingdom than religious people, without expecting any reward. And Jesus here takes the part of the last ones more than the first ones."

Because many are called, but few are chosen.

OLIVIA: "Lots of people would like to mail money to God in heaven, people who give alms in the temple like people buying insurance, without worrying about whether there's vaccines or medicines or if the people have enough to eat. And there are people who are going to die, who'll never have power, never get a job, they're just going to die; but they know they're going to free a lot of suffering people; and they're up in the mountains without anything; maybe they can't even read, and they're there like Christ suffering for the liberation of their country and of many countries, like Che who liberated one country and went to die in another. And this is what seems to me real Christianity, and those are the ones that Christ says are the chosen ones."

I said that in Aramaic "many" and "all" are the same, and when Christ says "many" he means "all." He's telling the Jews that all are called but few of them will be chosen. And here there are three judgments that Jesus makes of those religious people, each one stronger than the preceding one, and more radical. They perhaps were said on different occasions but the Evangelist has grouped them into a single text: first he tells them that those who are the last to work will receive the same as they do; then he tells them that the last ones will be ahead of them; then he tells them that few of them will be chosen.

"Is there anything more to add?"

"It's all very clear."

20.

The Curing of a Deaf Mute

(Mark 7:31–37)

Our little church is in a place where the island becomes very narrow, and we have the lake very close to us on both sides. Through the windows on the north side we look out at the lake slightly rippled and a grayish blue in color, and through the windows on the south side the lake is calm and sky blue.

I said the brief mention the Gospel makes of Jesus leaving Tyre and passing through Sidon and the Decapolis and returning to the lake means that he has been abroad, among the pagans, and he's possibly being persecuted and has been in a kind of exile. Part of the lake was occupied by the Decapolis, which were ten pagan tribes, and Jesus may have still been among pagans, and the deaf mute they bring him for the laying on of hands may also have been a pagan.

Jesus took him to one side, apart from the people,

*and he put his fingers in the man's ears
and he spat and he touched the man's tongue.*

BOSCO: "It sounds like quackery and witch-craft."

OSCAR: "What I don't understand is why he took him away from the group, why he did this all alone, separating him from the community."

DON TANO, from the opposite shore: "We have to decipher everything, right? He's telling us this for some reason. We have to try and understand it."

OSCAR: "Man, just think: when Jesus performed that miracle when he spat on his tongue, what would people think they were watching? I imagine he must have looked disgusted. He could have performed it some other way, couldn't he? Maybe he wanted to see if they had faith in him, and so he spat. But you know I'm disgusted by somebody else's saliva that drops on me; and to have somebody drip it on my tongue, spit on me, ugh! That would really be disgusting."

I: "I think Jesus spat on his finger and with his saliva-covered finger he touched the man's tongue."

RAUL: "But it was the saliva of the man, man!"

OSCAR: "Oh, sure, of course."

DONALD: "I think maybe Jesus took him aside to give him a special distinction. Maybe people didn't like that boy very much, because they look at deaf mutes like children; they don't take them seriously, don't pay them any attention. And the kids laugh at them. Everybody makes fun of the deaf. They talk to them, and since they don't hear and can't talk, they're useless."

LAUREANO: "Don't you believe it, those bastards are evil."

DONALD: "Do you know why they're evil? Because anything people say to them they think they're making fun of them, because they always do. I've seen them calling mutes sons-of-bitches and things like that, since they don't hear. But maybe later somebody says to them, maybe in writing: He called you such-and-such. And then they get mean and then they won't let you talk to them, that's why they don't want anybody to talk to them; they get them all mixed up. And, poor guy, it would be a lot of suffering for him, and then Jesus realizes this and he gives him special attention, taking him off to one side."

I: "As for what Bosco was saying, that it looked like quackery or witchcraft, maybe there was something of that. In ancient times people believed saliva had magic powers, and people still think so: here they put spit on the bait so the fish will bite better. Maybe Jesus wanted to show the healing power there was in him."

ALEJANDRO, who is in charge of giving out our medicines: "The Christians later were strongly inclined to a magic mentality, but it may have been a simpler thing, psychological or something like that. In addition to the saliva he may have chewed some root or some other stuff. As for all that magic, I don't agree. The fact is that he was a great leader, and if there's a great leader, especially in the country or in remote places, he has to do everything, even doctoring. He takes on teaching and everything. It was part of his conscientization work."

I: "They tell Jesus to lay hands on him. In those times that was also to cure. In the rite of extreme unction the priest still lays his hands on the sick person. Our friend the poet and doctor Fernando Silva believes strongly that you have to touch the patient. He also believes you can cure without being a doctor. He has told me that I should touch the sick and that this way I can cure a lot of people. I believe Alejandro practices that, and I've seen that without knowing medicine he makes admirable cures with whatever he prescribes, and people have a lot of faith in him."

> *Then Jesus looked up to heaven, sighing,*
> *and he said:*
> *"Ephphatha!" which means "Open."*

OLIVIA: "Looking up to heaven was a kind of prayer. He showed us that we must have confidence in the Father."

I: "The heaven of the astronauts was not the heaven of the Jews. For them heaven was a vault set up on columns or foundations and in which the sun moved, and the moon, and the stars. But there was also talk of various

heavens or of the heaven of heavens. Heaven
was God's dwelling, and also his throne. Jesus
tells us about our Father who is in heaven.
Matthew instead of using the word 'God' uses
the word 'heaven,' and so he says the kingdom
of heaven instead of the kingdom of God, and
he speaks of having a treasure in heaven instead of a treasure in God. Christ came from
heaven, and after his death he went up to
heaven and he will come down to judge on the
clouds of heaven. Saint Paul speaks of heaven
as a city or a community destined for us. In the
Apocalypse Saint John says that new heavens
and a new earth will be created, and the new
society, the new Jerusalem, will come down
from heaven. It was at this heaven that Jesus
looked and, according to Mark, he was sighing."

NATALIA, the Solentiname midwife: "Maybe
it was from distress, because when you have a
sick person on your hands, in trouble, you sigh
like that. You pretend, and you look again, and
you sigh! What wouldn't you give to know
more to help the person who's suffering. Just
the night before last I had a case like that: a
child almost dead. They brought her to me
yesterday at dawn. The woman was calling to
me, and I could hear the child screaming. 'Oh,'
I said, 'Julio, look out the window, I hear a
child crying.' He said: 'A light is coming along.'
And I opened the window and stuck my head
out, and I saw a man coming with a child all
stretched out, and I said: 'Oh, my God, what's
that?' 'Doña Natalia, Doña Natalia,' they

called. 'Here I am. What do you want?' 'This
poor child is dead and I want you to look at
her.' 'Well, let's see, and God's will be done.'
You know, I don't know a thing; I never
learned anything, either about doctoring or
anything else, but everything is in having
faith in me: if I do any little thing, maybe just
praying to God! So I got up and went out and
there she was with the girl all stretched out.
'Is she alive?' the man said to me. 'Yes,' I told
him, 'Yes she is. Don't you worry. Have faith in
God, because I'm going to give her a little
something.' And so I made up some medicine.
And after a while the girl began to move. And
what I did was nothing but since he had faith
maybe in me, and in God, the child recovered.
The truth was I didn't want to worry them but
I thought the girl was dead. And I sighed and
sighed, 'Oh, my God!' heartbroken to see a
mother there weeping. And that's the way
Jesus was sighing, I think."

IVAN: "And when he said, 'Open!' it wasn't
only that their ears should open but that they
should open themselves to other people."

BOSCO: "There are some people that have
ears but don't hear. All they hear are radios
that are nothing but ads and propaganda.
They're deaf and so they're dumb."

OLIVIA: "We can have good ears but they're
no good to us if our heart doesn't open up. It's
the whole person that he's telling to open up,
not just the ears, to sense the reality that he
wasn't sensing. And this is what he was coming to do with all of humanity. Our senses, too,

have been opened up on these islands and we're aware of injustice, which we didn't use to see."

FELIPE: "We're ignorant people, simple, humble, many of us are illiterate, without any training for talking, and we were like people really dumb. But now here in the church the people can hear and now they can express themselves too."

I: "Don't you think that in this community a miracle is being repeated?"

At this moment the ears of the deaf man opened,
and his tongue was healed and he could now talk well.

FATHER EDUARDO MEJIA, a friend who is visiting us: "I was here before, about six years ago, and at that time they scarcely dared to sing in church, much less say anything. And I've come back and now I see that this miracle has happened. I am a witness of the great change that has taken place here."

TOMAS: "We had our ears stopped up. That's good, they must have thought. Because the truth is that those of us who used to come here, we couldn't even remotely say anything. And those of us who began to speak, we didn't know what we were saying. So we began, and we go ahead, our senses opening up more and more, as we hear more and more."

I: "This must encourage the ones that aren't talking yet."

TOMAS: "Maybe the ones that don't talk know the most."

OSCAR: "We must admit, Ernesto, that Jesus Christ has done this: I was a man that maybe had something important to say, and I didn't say it out of fear. But it seems that Jesus Christ performed the miracle and without realizing it he even spat on my tongue so that I could talk without any hesitation and hear what they were saying to me. If I understand and if I talk it seems to me it's because he spat on my tongue and I didn't even realize it. He performed the miracle."

PANCHO: "But it doesn't mean we all should be talking like parrots in a mango tree."

FELIPE: "Friend Pancho, don't you think that if we all talked, even though it was only one little word, this meeting would seem livelier?"

PANCHO: "Lively, sure, but we'd be here until six in the afternoon."

And Jesus ordered them not to tell anyone, but the more he ordered them, the more they told about it.

FELIPE: "I think Jesus said that because of the repression, which was already in existence at that time."

BOSCO: "Maybe that's why he took him off to one side. He wanted to help the guy, but he didn't want them to know it and to proclaim him the Messiah."

I: "He wanted to work in the dark, but what

he was doing became known and the more he said not to talk about it the more they talked. This was dangerous for him, but he had to take the risk of facing that danger, and that finally brought him to his death."

And they were much amazed and they said:
"He does everything well;
he even makes the deaf hear and the dumb
*   talk."*

FELIPE: "It's the poor little people, the common people that go around saying that. They're grateful for what he's done for them."

OLIVIA: "The people that were already aware, that already had their ears open and their tongues loose. They weren't the powerful, because to the powerful the liberation of the people is not a good thing."

MYRIAM, one of Olivia's daughters: "And it seems to me that the people that said Jesus did everything well said it knowing that he was going to end up dying for what he was doing."

TOMAS: "And they also realized that he was coming to change things. They thought, we're not going to have any more sick people, we're not going to have any more deaf or dumb, we're all going to be healthy now. When they saw him die they lost heart. But then they saw him resurrected and everything became the same again. We've realized that he goes on performing miracles."

OSCAR: "Ernesto, well, I don't know. Maybe I've been drinking too much. I feel myself inspired. It seems to me that these people were saying that what he was doing was good, but they had doubts: I can't explain why, but it seems to me that there were still doubts; he might be the Messiah, the liberator, or he might not. But now we have no doubts about who he is, and that he performed these miracles, the ones we're hearing about, the ones we're talking about now."

21.

The Good Shepherd

(John 10:7–16)

I began by saying that in ancient times the kings and political leaders—not the religious leaders—were called "shepherds" or "pastors." Homer calls the kings "pastors of men." And so they are called in the Bible; on the other hand, the Bible never calls priests and prophets pastors. The prophet Ezekiel says of the leaders of Israel that they are shepherds who drink the milk, dress in the wool, and eat the fattest sheep. That's why the sheep have been scattered and lost in the hills. Yahweh will take the sheep from their mouths, and he himself will be their shepherd; he will gather them together. "Flock" at that time meant "people."

> *I tell you truly: I am the door through which*
> *the sheep enter.*
> *All those who came before me are thieves and*
> *bandits;*
> *but the sheep paid them no heed.*

GIGI, our Peruvian friend: "Because everybody had a power that they'd taken by force; and they ruled by means of a social class that had imposed itself on the others through a private appropriation of the means of production and through the system of slavery of that time."

MANUEL: "And those who were going to come after him were going to be thieves and bandits too. He says he's the only one who isn't."

"And that includes David and Solomon?"

WILLIAM: "If not, he would have made the qualification."

FELIPE: "He says all governments were thieves, and still are, because their laws are to protect private property: robbery."

TOMAS: "And they kill, too, because not to give the workers what is due them is like killing, killing little by little, a little every day, it seems to me."

ALEJO: "And it's clear that, as he says, the people paid no heed to them. If they gave in to them it was by force; they didn't give in out of love, but because they were obliged to."

FELIPE: "The people weren't for Herod; the people weren't for Caesar; but they *were* for Jesus, the poor people."

ELVIS: "I'll give another example, the fascist military junta of Chile, which is hated by everybody. The people can't be for them."

ALEJANDRO: "And if he's saying, 'All those who came before me,' it's because he considers himself a political boss, a *leader*."

I: "Our word 'líder' comes from English 'leader,' and means 'guide,' something very close to 'shepherd.' So we can say that this is the Parable of the Good Leader."

GIGI: "And what a revolutionary that Jesus is, condemning all the previous political systems, saying they were thieves and bandits! According to the ideas of that time those political systems were legal and even of divine origin."

I: "But what Jesus thinks about the kings is the same as the Bible thought. When Israel wants to be 'like the other nations' and have a king, Yahweh speaks to them through the prophet Samuel, telling them that the king will make their sons drive his wagons and cultivate his fields, and will make their daughters hairdressers and cooks and bakers, and will take away from them their vineyards and olive orchards to give them to his officials. But Israel insists on being like the other nations and on having a king. And with the kings it happened just as Samuel had prophesied, even with David, who took Uriah's wife away and ordered him slain, and with Solomon, who had a thousand wives, and it's because every king is a thief and bandit."

I am the good shepherd.
The good shepherd gives his life for his sheep;
but the one that works only for pay,
when he sees the wolf coming,
he leaves the sheep and flees,
because he is not the shepherd

and because the sheep are not his.
Then the wolf seizes the sheep and scatters
   them.

MANUEL: "Some in the government are getting rich, and others are giving their lives for their brothers and sisters."

WILLIAM: "And what is the wolf? It seems to me the wolf is exploitation: the one who instead of being a person towards people is a wolf towards people."

GIGI: "He says the wolf seizes the sheep and scatters them: because exploitation divides people into classes. And the exploitation system in society creates individualism and selfishness, prevents humankind from living in communion."

TOMAS: "We're all scattered."

NATALIA: "To live in unity we have to live in equality. Here we've got well dressed *campesinos*, and it seems to me that we're all equal."

MANUEL: "The corral is to gather the cattle. And he has come to gather humanity, which was scattered, each one going in a different direction. It seems to me that the corral is his church."

GIGI: "But that stuff about the bad shepherds can also apply to the religious pastors, not just the politicians, when they enjoy political power together with the politicians and get fat with the sheep."

"The ruler must be like Jesus, a good shepherd; he must do like (and this will surprise a lot of people), like Fidel Castro has done. I don't know him and I don't know much about him, but I've heard about him some. A lot of people say he's a communist bastard that doesn't believe in God. I don't care if he believes in God. You know what I do care about? That he's aware of things and wants to give love. And to give his body for others, for his people. That's what Christ did, you understand? Now, not just Fidel Castro, but lots of people who have died: I don't need to say their names. You understand, a lot of us understand who are the dead that will always live in our hearts."

I am the good shepherd.
I know my sheep and my sheep know me,
just as my Father knows me and I know my
*   Father.*
And I give my life for my sheep.

DONALD: "The good shepherds or the good leaders aren't dictators in offices. They know their people and their people know them."

OLIVIA: "And Jesus says that just as he knows his people, he knows his Father. It's a single knowledge."

I: "In the Bible 'knowledge' is the same as 'love.' "

GIGI: "Christ appears as a link between the people and love (and God). And he says the people know him: the people know love through him. 'They know me' means they know his message of mutual love. That is, everybody knows that with love they'll live happy, with love the world will be better, without the selfishness and the anti-social forces that have governed them."

I: "The people know love, as you say. Because if Christ knows the Father, who is love, and the people know Christ, they know love. Christ and the people and love (God) are all the same thing."

> *I also have other sheep who are not of this fold;*
> *I have to bring them also.*
> *They will obey me,*
> *and there will be a single flock and a single shepherd.*

"Those are probably some sheep that aren't tame, that are wild ones."

I: "I don't think they're wild; they just aren't from this sheepfold. He says they're his sheep and they're in other folds. It's as if he said: 'Beside the Christian church that you know, I have other churches.'"

A gentleman from San Carlos: "It seems to me that he's referring to other sects, like the Adventists or Evangelicals, that aren't in the same fold as his church but they're going to be."

FELIPE: "It seems to me that what Jesus cared about was love and not whether or not they belonged to a religious sect. When he says he has others, he's saying he has others that

love, that know him and that know love, and
he's not thinking that there are others who
happen to be praying or singing."

OLIVIA: "It's all the people who weren't
Christian, but still belonged to him because
they were good people. He's referring to the
good people everywhere."

WILLIAM: "What has happened in Mao's
China—putting an end to hunger, to prostitution, to ignorance, to the frightful misery
there used to be, and giving everyone great
dignity and enough food, clothing, medicines,
education, amusements—that's like another
church of Christ, with another name."

I: "And what he says about a single flock and
a single shepherd is that all humanity is going
to unite, and there's going to be a single
leader, who is Christ: the word of love."

"All humanity, even the exploiters?"

WILLIAM: "The exploiters are the enemies of
humanity, the wolves that can't be with the
flock. He says all the sheep are going to be
united in a single flock with a single shepherd,
but he doesn't say with the wolves."

FRANCISCO: "The one who's a wolf to others
will have to stop being a wolf to be with the
sheep; otherwise the Good Shepherd won't
allow him in the flock."

GIGI: "What he said is very revolutionary
and it's still revolutionary even now in the
twentieth century: that there are many of his
people outside the church."

WILLIAM: "And it's also very revolutionary,

what he says, that he'll form a single people with his church and with all the people that don't belong to his church."

GIGI: "And he's saying it at a time when, for the Jews, everything functioned around religion."

"He's saying that he's going to unite Christians and Marxists."

"To make a single revolution."

GIGI: "And he's also putting an end to nationalism, at a time when the Jews had a religious nationalism or a nationalist religion: telling them that out of all the other nations he's going to make a single people."

WILLIAM: "As if to say proletarian internationalism."

GIGI: "How different is this picture of the Good Shepherd that we've been shown here from the little religious pictures: an effeminate Jesus carrying a little lamb on his shoulders."

OLIVIA: "Those who aren't of his church 'will obey me,' he says. And that means they will obey the commandment of love. And that's why humanity is going to be a single flock with a single shepherd because humanity is going to be united by love."

IVAN: "That single flock and that single king will come when we've established perfect communism."

I: "A world-wide revolution with a single leader, or a single king as they said at that time."

22.

The "Wicked Wealth"

(Luke 16:1–15)

Some Managua capitalists have just bought a great stretch of land in Solentiname. They came to see it with a group of friends, and on Sunday some of those people also came to visit our community and attended Mass. On this occasion we also had with us our friend Dionisio, the young Costa Rican communist.

The Gospel for this Sunday was about the dishonest manager. He realizes he's going to be fired from his job and he calls in his master's debtors; the one that owed a hundred barrels of oil got his debt reduced to fifty, and the one that owed five tons of wheat got his debt reduced to four, so that when he was fired he would have friends that would treat him well.

And the master praised the bad manager because he had been clever to act like that. For the children of this world are more clever

in dealing with one another than the
children of light.
I recommend that you use wicked wealth to
make friends,
so that when the wealth is gone
there will be people to receive you into the
eternal dwellings.

TOMAS PEÑA: "So it means it's not a sin to rob a rich man if he's about to give you something. That's how it is, right?"

OLIVIA: "That's an example that he gives to tell us we have to give the riches that we have to win friends in the kingdom of heaven. This is a kind of parable. And he means also that the riches of the rich don't really belong to them. They don't have them for long; nobody has them beyond death, so giving them away is like giving away what doesn't belong to you."

OSCAR: "I see it this way: that man, what he was really doing was stealing. He got himself some friends with his master's money and what the master said was that he was a very clever thief. And Jesus tells this parable to the rich to make them see that they are thieves; they're not the real owners, they're the managers of other people's wealth, but they're like that servant that disposed of other people's wealth as if it was their own. And what Jesus says is: be clever thieves, that is, be clever rich people, and the money you've got give it to the poor so you'll be saved."

JULIO: "He's not saying then like Tomás

says that you have to steal to give to the poor; he's saying that rich people's money is stolen money and that stolen money they ought to give to the poor."

OSCAR: "That's good. Notice that guy did a good thing there: he turned thief on his master but he earned the friendship of other people."

A lady of the capitalist group: "That man shouldn't have mismanaged the money, and then they wouldn't have fired him and then he would have been even more clever."

Another capitalist: "If he had stolen only for himself and not for the others and if he'd been saving what he was stealing at the time when they fired him he wouldn't have grieved or had to seek favors from anyone, and so he'd have also been more clever."

Another member of this group, a cousin of mine, an ex-priest: "This is a parable. And it seems to me that what Christ wanted to do through it was to give a new projection to money. The servant could have kept the hundred barrels and all the wheat, but what he did was to help others. So he shows us that money can also be used to do good to others. Even though that man didn't do it to do good to others but to win friends. So with money you can give alms, and if you share with others you win more friends here on earth; and when you die you'll also have those friendships in heaven, with those people you gave alms to. So you can win heaven with money."

OLIVIA: "It seems to me it's a parable, a way of speaking, that we must understand in accordance with the rest of the Gospel. The Gospel is always against possessing wealth; it has always said it should be shared. Somewhere else it says: 'If you want to follow me, give away everything you have and then follow me.' And it seems to me that in this parable he's saying you have to be intelligent, that you don't give alms to get friends, or heaven (a selfish heaven), you give everything away so that everyone together can enjoy the kingdom of heaven."

FELIPE: "To be received in that brotherly society of love—that's what the kingdom of heaven is."

OSCAR: "What he did with other people's wealth is what the rich ought to do with their own wealth, give it away."

LAUREANO: "Well, what they think is their own isn't their own; it's also other people's."

I: "That's why Jesus, the two times he mentions wealth here, calls it 'wicked' (in other translations it's called 'unjust,' 'cursed,' 'sinful,' which is the same thing). And this isn't an adjective to refer only to a certain kind of wealth, as if there were other kinds that were just; it refers to all wealth, because all wealth is unjust, all is stolen."

MANUEL: "In other words, he's telling the rich that they're all thieves, but as long as they're thieves, then let them be intelligent thieves: let them share the wealth before death takes it away from them."

FELIPE: "Or the revolution."

I continued: "And it's interesting what Porfirio Miranda says in his book _Marx and the Bible:_ that the Bible often, for the word 'alms' uses the Hebrew word 'justice,' in the sense of doing justice, restoring, returning. That's why Christ also calls all wealth unjust, because it's stolen. You ought to divide it because it isn't yours, it belongs to others. And this is also the thought of all the church fathers. Saint Basil says that the rich are owners of the common wealth because they were the first to seize it. Saint John Chrysostom says that the rich do not enjoy what is theirs but what belongs to others. Saint Jerome says that every rich man is a thief or the heir of a thief."

> _Those who are honest with little will be honest with much;_
> _and those who are not honest with little will not be honest with much either._
> _If, then, with wicked wealth you are not honest_
> _who will entrust to you true wealth?_
> _And if you are not honest with the wealth of others_
> _who is going to give you what belongs to you?_

Another one from the Managua group: "But here he condemns theft, when he speaks of those who do not treat honestly what belongs to others."

I: "What the Gospel here calls 'what belongs to others' is what the rich consider as their property. It says that we won't receive our own (the kingdom of heaven) if we haven't been honest with other people's property. One is honest with wealth when one doesn't appropriate it for oneself but distributes it among its legitimate owners. In capitalism, robbery is taking private property from someone. In socialism, robbery is wanting to keep as private property what belongs to everyone; and so it is also in the Gospels: that's why Christ calls wealth 'unjust' (stolen)."

MARCELINO: "And it also says that if we've not been honest with unjust wealth, we won't be given the true wealth. True wealth is love. If we have stolen wealth, false wealth, and we don't distribute it, we won't get the true wealth, love, because love is received only by people who give. If you're rich in money you're poor in love."

REBECA, his wife: "And it says if you're not honest with little, you won't be honest with much: little are those riches of the rich; great are the riches of the kingdom, love."

One of the Managua visitors: "But if we distribute what belongs to others we're not behaving honestly. If we distribute what belongs to others, as if those things belonged to us, we're no longer being so honest."

I: "The rich people who distribute their riches can't be very honest because the riches aren't theirs; they belong to the people (and in the parable the example given is of a manager who wasn't honest), but they can be intelligent. Because if they do this, they'll be received in the kingdom of heaven. Otherwise it will be the people that will forcibly distribute those riches, and it won't be robbery because they belonged to the people. But this last matter isn't discussed in this parable, it's discussed in other Gospel passages, like that one that says that the Son of Man will come 'like a thief in the night.' "

A visiting lady: "So according to this there's nothing that belongs to others; everything belongs to everyone, and you have to distribute it all, whether you like it or not?"

My cousin: "That would take away liberty, which is an essential value for Christianity. God has created us free; we can be sinners if we wish, and he will not oblige us by force to be good. And if the rich are obliged by force to distribute their riches, their action would have no merit."

I: "The freedom that we must take away is the freedom to exploit, the freedom to take away the freedom of others. Just because God made us free, no one is free to make us slaves. As for merit, it is clear that the rich have no merit if they distribute by force: therefore they must do it voluntarily."

DIONISIO: "Like that manager that distributed what wasn't his. All of it wasn't his, although maybe a part of it was, what he'd produced with his own work. But what catches my attention is this: this parable is for the rich, and Christ doesn't give an example of a rich man but of a manager. It seems to me that it's to show that the rich man is only a manager of money. In the parable the owner of the money also appears. But the owner of the wealth is God, or the people, which is the same thing, but not the rich. And the meaning of the parable, it seems to me, is that the rich mustn't be fools, that the day is coming, and soon, when they'll be stripped, and they'd better be a willing part of the action. It's an invitation to the rich to be revolutionaries. And it seems to me that Christ tells them this, individually, because some of them can change, although as a class they're not going to change. There have been bourgeois revolutionaries, like Engels, an owner of textile factories. The rich must be intelligent like that, being revolutionaries. And the poor must also be intelligent, distributing the expropriated wealth revolutionarily, and not with a bourgeois mentality of private appropriation, of selfishness and of individualism."

FELIPE: "It shouldn't be that, as this parable also says, the people of darkness are brighter than the people of light."

DIONISIO: "God created the world (or else the revolution did it, which is the same thing) for everybody. With plants, animals, birds, fish, and all natural resources, for all people. But they sinned by falling into the temptation of selfishness; that was the sinful fruit that they ate, wanting to have things for themselves or for their little group, and they appropriated for themselves what belonged to everybody and private property appeared."

I: "Dionisio belongs to the Communist Youth in his country, but what he has said is the same thing that the fathers of the church said:

that in paradise everything is owned in common and that with sin private property was introduced."

A young lady from the Managua group, speaking softly: "But there were some people who worked more and obtained more things, while others stood around with arms crossed waiting for things to fall down out of the sky, and that's where the inequalities come from. So what we have to do is all work equally so that we'll all have equally. Let everything belong to everyone, but obtained with the effort of everyone. And let's not want to go without working, without making an effort, waiting for the distribution of the things produced by those who have worked."

Another of the Managua group: "Then everybody would get rich."

The young lady, very softly: "But everyone ought to make an effort. If my neighbor was the one that worked himself to death, the one that was lively and intelligent and who profited and could achieve his ambition, and I didn't: then I can't complain."

DIONISIO: speaking very softly, as Costa Ricans do: "The young lady raises a good point: nobody should be left without work and take advantage of the work of others. That's precisely what shouldn't exist."

OLIVIA: "The rich person is the one who just directs the work and receives the profits from it; the one who does it is the worker, the *campesino*, the stupid one, the illiterate, the one who doesn't have any education and so is

used like an ox. Then it means that the humble
people, the poor people, are the ones that
create the wealth. It's the mass of the poor, the
majority, that has created that wealth enjoyed by a few."

I: "Of course. All the wealth on earth has
been created by the workers. The clothes that
we have on were made by workers; the shoes
we walk in were made by other workers; the
food we eat was produced by workers in the
field; the houses we live in, and even the great
skyscrapers in the cities, and the highways
and the bridges, we owe to the workers. But
there are people who have a lot of things without ever having made clothes, without having
made a shoe, without having sown a seed,
without having laid a brick, without having
produced a single thing of value on earth.
They consume a lot, because the class that
doesn't produce is the class that consumes
most; most of the goods are consumed by them,
the ones that don't work. In natural history
those are called parasites. A parasite is an
organism that lives at another's expense,
feeding on the substance of the other."

The young lady from Managua: "But probably that person had an idea and with it created
a whole stream of work."

I: "The parasite also has work, a parasite's
work. And exploiters can believe that they
also work, and even that they work themselves to death, but it's not productive work;
it's the work of extracting the profits from the

work of others, the work of making others work. A vampire also has to make an effort, sucking blood."

DIONISIO: "To come closer to home, I'm going to talk about my family. On my father's side we're dirt poor, but on my mother's side, my grandparents and my uncles and aunts own land and textile factories. And I look at my cousins (not with resentment, I'm perfectly happy to be what I am), how they go to good schools, and then to Harvard or England, and they've got their good life guaranteed forever, and they've already got an inheritance of factories and estates that get bigger and bigger (they must be well managed). In a textile factory, the INTEX, for example, the workers receive wages of 600 to 900 *colones.* The rent on a tiny house, with only one room, is 400 *colones.* And I see the houses that my uncles and aunts live in. You can imagine the mansions they have. And I say to myself, how is it possible for men and women to work as they work (because they work very hard) and to live as they live, starving to death. Because a family can't live on 600 *colones;* and 600 *colones* is a generous salary, some people pay less. And my cousins have never known what work is; they've never touched a loom, they think that work is seeing to it that people work. That's not work; work is transforming raw material. And it's so obvious that that is exploitation, and my cousins don't know it."

My cousin: "I'm not wholly in agreement

with that concept of work. Because the buildings that the workers built also needed a plan."

I: "There is such a thing as intellectual work. But the capitalist that just puts up capital, and doesn't do any work, is exploiting."

A lady from Managua: "The capitalist gentleman who didn't work, who only put up his capital, he also contributed to production, because if he hadn't put up his capital, nothing would have been done."

DIONISIO: "That's true, in this capitalist society, because in it without money nothing gets done. But the point is to find out the origin of the money."

The president of the Managua Chamber of Commerce: "I have visited the Soviet Union and I have seen that there is quite a lot of capitalism there. They have even brought in American companies like the Ford Motor Company and Coca Cola. I suppose that kind of socialism is probably not your goal, that is, the goal of the Gospel."

I: "The goal of the Gospel is the perfect communist society, as Marx defined it: 'From each according to his abilities, to each according to his needs.' That's the society in which the first Christians lived when Christianity still had all its purity, as is told in the Acts of the Apostles: 'All those who had believed were very united and owned everything in common. They would sell their goods and all their property and they would divide the money to each one according to his needs' (Acts 2:44–45)."

A Managua lady, with a certain sarcasm: "We're assuming that we've reached a state of perfection in which we are free of all selfishness."

I: "That's why Christ came to earth, to establish that society of love, his kingdom. That's why he talks a lot about social life and economy. In this passage he talks to us of wealth: that it must be shared. In the following verse he tells us that 'one cannot serve God and money.' It's because God is love, and you can't have love and selfishness at the same time."

Another of the Managua ladies: "There are some people who carry out more important tasks, because they have better intellectual training, and they should be paid better than those who have an inferior intellectual training. Intellectual work has been better paid for centuries."

DIONISIO: "Sure, of course. You're right about that. Intellectual work pays better. But the bad thing is that many have no access to intellectual training because of the faulty distribution of the wealth. It seems to me that Nicaraguan illiteracy is enormous, and this results in a great mass of the people being enslaved. And the cause of it is private ownership of the means of production, which creates that difference among human beings."

Another visitor from Managua: "Perhaps it could be said that according to the Gospel the revolutionary is the child of light. But it seems that the Gospel is advising the revolutionaries to adopt the very methods of the capitalists, to be as clever as the exploiters."

I: "Just as they are diligent toward money, we must be diligent toward love. Just as they are efficient in exploitation, we must be efficient in distributing goods fraternally. Christ calls some men children of darkness, others, children of light. The whole universe has been formed from light, or from energy, which is the same thing. And the darkness is the same as the void. The children of the light are those who are in the line of the evolution of the universe, those who are continuing the process of creation, the supporters of life, in short: those who love. The children of the shadows are those of anti-evolution, the reactionaries, the supporters of death, those who do not love. The love that they devote to money, we must devote to God (or other people, which is the same thing), because as it says in the following verse: You cannot serve two masters, God and money. We commented on this verse in another Gospel passage, and besides, after all we have said here, it doesn't need any commentary."

You brag of being just in people's eyes,
but God knows your hearts.
And what people consider to be great,
God abhors.

I: "What people 'consider to be great' is all power, all domination, all authority, which God abhors because he is the spirit of revolution. He is against all control of some people by others. And private ownership of the means of production, as Dionisio says, or of wealth, as the Gospel says, is the reason why some people control others."

CESAR: "And the rich person who sees a change coming in the world (and you see it coming if you read the Gospels) and doesn't take steps to be admitted into the just society that's going to come, into the new humanity that's not going to die (which is what eternal dwelling places means), that person is acting like an idiot."

23.

The Kingdom of Heaven and Violence

(Matthew 11:12–19 and Luke 16:16–17)

From the time of the coming of John the Baptist until now,
the kingdom of heaven has suffered violence,
and those who use force try to seize the kingdom.

I said that at first I hadn't wanted us to comment on this verse because it seemed to me that you couldn't comment on it. The specialists in the scriptures say it's impossible to know what Jesus meant, because the Greek wording is ambiguous, and if we don't know what Jesus meant by the violence of the kingdom of heaven, then how are we going to comment on it? That's why, when we commented some time ago on the passage about the envoys of John the Baptist, we got only to the verse just before this one. They say this is the most obscure verse in the whole Bible.

218

Specialists say that in the Greek phrase you can't tell if the verb is active or passive, if the kingdom of heaven creates violence, or suffers violence, or even if violence is to be taken as good or evil. There are some who say (and this has been the traditional interpretation) that to conquer the kingdom of heaven you must do violence to yourself; but why this is so only since the coming of John the Baptist is not explained by this interpretation. Others say it means the kingdom of heaven is violent because it erupts with force, and because it comes to destroy the existing order. Others say it means that since the coming of John the Baptist a violence has been unloosed against the kingdom of heaven, the violence of the persecutors. Others say it means that, since the coming of John the Baptist, the zealots, the ones belonging to the army of armed struggle, were being converted to the new movement of the kingdom of heaven, as in the case of Peter and other disciples who were zealots. And others say it means that the zealots, the guerrilla fighters, mistakenly wanted to establish the kingdom of heaven by force of arms. Which interpretation are we left with? Are we going to choose arbitrarily the one we prefer? It's hard to comment when we don't know exactly what it means. But at any rate, I now wanted to see if we can comment on it.

There was a long silence. I read the verse again, slowly, so that we could reflect. I then continued:

"It seems to me that the idea that the vio-

lent ones that conquer the kingdom are the
ones that do violence to themselves by means
of asceticism, with sacrifices, penitence, and
fasting, doing violence to their natures in
every way, that idea we should reject. It has
been the traditional interpretation for many
centuries, but Jesus didn't talk about such
things. Instead, right here, a few verses later,
Jesus contrasts the lifestyle of John the Baptist (who 'neither ate nor drank'), with his own
life style (who 'eats and drinks, and you say
he's a glutton and a drunkard'). That's the
individualistic and purely spiritualistic interpretation of people who don't want to in-
terpret the Gospel politically. It seems to me
that he must be talking about political violence: either the political violence of the kingdom of heaven or that of the guerrilla fighters,
who in one way or another want to enter the
kingdom, with arms or by laying down arms, or
the violence of the enemies of the kingdom of
heaven: Herod, the Sanhedrin, the Romans."

We had with us our friend the poet ANTIDIO
CABAL, who had come from Venezuela. He
was the father of Dionisio, who had been here
before, and the husband of the poet Mayra
Jiménez. He said, speaking slowly: "Well,
sticking strictly to the text, I'd say there was a
reaction against the kingdom of heaven from
the moment when John the Baptist appears."

I interrupted: "He was in prison, and they
were soon going to slaughter him."

ANTIDIO: "That's why: it means that John
the Baptist brought something new with re-

spect to the kingdom of heaven. The kingdom was accepted up until he arrived, it seems. When he arrived, something new was introduced. This newness will be the antagonism it produced in the authorities. It seems that what John said or did wasn't agreeable to the men who in some way governed relations with God. Now, well I'm not sure about this, about what I'm going to say, because the text isn't clear either in one sense or in the other. It could be understood, or maybe not, that they're talking about two kinds of violence. He says: 'Up to now, the kingdom of heaven has suffered violence'; and later he says: 'Those who use force try to seize it.' It seems that it is a question of two violences, the violence brought by John, who understands the kingdom of heaven in a way different from how it was formerly understood; and the violence of people who have power, the power of arms and money, that is, authority, and who are opposed to the renewal that John the Baptist brings. This is another possible interpretation. The two times that you've read the text, explaining it right away, it's seemed to me that you identify the first, 'violence,' with the second, 'force.' It could be, or maybe it couldn't be."

I: "That's what I was doing just now. Probably Christ left it ambiguous because he wanted to, and he wanted to talk about the two violences. Only a moment ago I was thinking why it is, as some say that this text hasn't been understood down through the centuries. Up to now we haven't found anything in the Bible that we've failed to understand. Maybe he wanted to introduce it like that, mysteriously, so we'd discuss it as we're discussing it today and so we'd keep in mind the violence of liberation and that of the oppressors. He must be talking, as Antidio says, about the two violences."

ANTIDIO: "It seems that Jesus is talking here about violence and force. There's the *violence* of people who want to change what is evil, and the *force* of the establishment that tries to prevent things from changing."

I: "It may be appropriate to say here what I read in the commentary of a scripture scholar: the word 'to seize' that is used here in Greek has a meaning applied especially to spoils of war. It's to make off with the spoils; it's to seize, rob, grab in order to distribute. And that's what they want to do, 'the ones who use force' with the kingdom of heaven."

ANTIDIO: "What follows might clarify things a little, up to a certain point."

All the prophets and the law of Moses spoke of the kingdom until John came.

ANTIDIO, clearly and slowly: "The prophets and the law of Moses spoke of the kingdom ... until John came. From then on, force tries to prevent the establishment of the kingdom. There are two different situations with respect to the kingdom: from the prophets and Moses until John appears, and from John on."

MAYRA, Antidio's wife: "It occurs to me, Ernesto, that perhaps John brings a new concept of the kingdom of heaven (a kingdom of heaven that is the bringing about of perfect equality and justice on earth) and that necessarily creates violence: a violence in the first place within ourselves, and an external violence that wants to take possession of heaven and snatch heaven from us like a prize of war."

I: " 'The prophets and the law of Moses' in the time of Jesus meant what we now understand by the Old Testament. Jesus is saying that the prophetic books and the five books of the Pentateuch attributed to Moses (the whole Bible) *talked* of the kingdom: they announced it as a future kingdom. Until John. From then on, the kingdom has been a reality. Jesus didn't come to change anything about the law and the prophets; he says somewhere else that he does not come to change the law but to carry it out. This is the law of the Bible, which is none other than the law of love. The revolutionary Bible writer José Porfirio Miranda makes it clear that Jesus didn't bring any new message. He said absolutely nothing new, nothing different from what the prophets said. For the prophets and Jesus the kingdom is the same one: a just, perfect society: Communism on earth. The difference is that the prophets were announcing the future kingdom, and Jesus says that it has already arrived; that is his new tidings. And the new tidings of John, the precursor, who said that the kingdom was 'near.' "

JULIO CASTILLA, a worker from Juigalpa:

"John told them something really screwy: now is the hour for change."

I: "He told them: 'Now is the revolution.' And that's why since John came violence came. Earlier, when they talked about the kingdom, there was no conflict. They talked about a future society. Now we must expropriate private property and all that, and now comes violence. The violence that we ourselves must make, and the external violence, as Mayra says."

ANTIDIO: "This is an example that I want to give now, because earlier I was talking conceptually. It's what we've seen in Cuba. I was saying that violence is the violence of the guerrilla fighters, and the force is the force of the government that wants things to continue as they are, in opposition to the changes that the guerrilla fighters want to make. We could also say that violence is a kind of force that wants to change an unjust situation, while force is a kind of violence that doesn't want an unjust situation to change. The first represents the renewers, and a contemporary figure is Fidel Castro; it's constructive, positive violence, and the violence of justice, that exists only because of the existence of the force that is the violence of injustice. It's what is happening right now. The kingdom of heaven has to adapt now to this new historical situation: justice conquered by violence, in accordance with this text. So we're referring, with this language, to a current political and social situation, right now, which exists in many

countries in the Americas and in other parts of
the world, but which comes from John the
Baptist."

I: "Christ was talking of the kingdom of
heaven as something that was soon going to be
established. I've often asked myself why it
hasn't yet been established. It seems to me
that it's because he came in the midst of a
slave society, and before the establishment of
the kingdom, humanity has to pass through
several stages. If he had come now, the kingdom, that society, would come into being
quickly. But if he hadn't come at that time we
wouldn't have the social progress we now
have. He had to come in the midst of a slave
society, and die crucified in that society. And
thanks to him the kingdom of heaven has come
close to us. Martí said that humanity has
climbed half of Jacob's ladder. And since Martí
it's advanced even more. Especially in Cuba. I
believe this has been much clarified for us by
what Antidio has said, that it's no longer as
obscure as the Bible scholars said it was, and
that we can comment on it."

ESPERANZA: "Ernesto, I see that what
Christ says began to exist with John the Baptist is the same thing that has begun to exist
with us with the Gospel. We had religion, a lot
of religion throughout the country, but it
didn't mean a thing. Only now, when we're
beginning to discover the Gospel in all its passages, does it have to bring violence because of
course it goes against the rich. So it's something violent because the rich are not about to

let their things be taken from them. So each part of the Gospel brings violence, which we have to create, then, even if we don't want it."

I: "What Esperanza says is as clear as a bell. At first the Gospel didn't bring any danger; they even thought that the kingdom of heaven was the sky. But with John and Christ, of course, violence already begins, revolutionary violence, and counterrevolutionary violence."

OLIVIA: "And you could also say: the violence of love and the violence of injustice, those are the two violences. Because there is a just violence, a violence of love that wants to put an end to injustice with the Gospel, with love among people."

I: "So what Christ is saying is that the prophets talked about the kingdom, but that's all they did, just talked. Now is the time for action. Now there is revolution and repression."

OLIVIA: "But revolutionary violence exists to put an end once and for all to all violence and to bring love into being."

I: "If the violent were the ascetics, those who do violence to themselves, it's hard to understand how they can seize the kingdom of heaven, since the kingdom of heaven isn't heaven the way we used to think about it; it's a perfect society. How can good people, saints, want to seize a society and appropriate it for themselves? But if the kingdom of heaven is a society, as we know it is, it certainly *is* clear that those who use force do want to take it away from us."

ANTIDIO: "I'm going to add something. I've been rereading this text, and it makes it very clear that the coming of the kingdom of heaven isn't once and for all but something that gradually gets done, and this kind of violence assumes that it's something hard to achieve. And when it says that those who use force try to conquer it, I start thinking that Christianity has been conquered by that force for two thousand years, not counting the two or three hundred years of primitive Christianity. This kingdom that they're trying to build was blocked by the people who had the force, who were rulers of the world (of weapons, of money, and of culture). They have opposed Christ's plan to establish justice. Injustice was perpetuated. You could say they snatched the kingdom and they've kept it snatched for seventeen hundred years, that kingdom of heaven. That kingdom would have already come if we humans had wanted it."

JULIO: "The kingdom of heaven is perfect communism."

IVAN: "And John's role was to be the precursor of that society."

And if you are willing to believe it,
John is the prophet Elijah, who was destined
*   to come.*
Those who have ears, let them listen.

I: "For the Jews, the cycle of the prophets had already ended. There couldn't be any more prophets than those of the biblical canon. But it was also believed that the prophet Elijah, who according to legend had not died but had been swept up in a chariot of fire, would return to earth before the Messiah came. That was the last word of Malachi, the last of the prophets according to the biblical canon. At the time of Christ there was what we may call a great devotion for Elijah, the greatest prophet of the Old Testament, a prophet and a martyr. They were expecting him. According to the scribes Jesus couldn't be the Messiah because Elijah hadn't returned. Jesus answered that line of thought by saying that the prophet Elijah had already arrived in the person of John the Baptist (who was not a new prophet because there couldn't be any more prophets; the hour of the kingdom had come). But he specified: 'If you *are willing* to believe it, John is the prophet Elijah.' He was Elijah only on the condition that they accepted him. According to Malachi, Elijah was going to come to reconcile humanity. Today we'd say to put an end to class distinctions. Later, when they'd already killed John the Baptist, Jesus said: 'It is true that Elijah is coming first, and that he will arrange everything. But I say to you that Elijah already came and they did not recognize him but did to him whatever they wanted.' Here Jesus adds that anyone with ears should listen, and this also means that it depends on them whether John is Elijah. I've also read that 'those who have ears, let them listen' was a Jewish refrain that was repeated when an obscure ruling was being put forward."

FELIPE: "That means those who are aware."

OSCAR: "It means we shouldn't be stupid, man."

JULIO: "It means that Elijah has to keep coming. Marx too could have been another Elijah, if we're willing to believe."

I: "Those who are in favor of change, then, those who are ready to accept this, they accept it. The others are going to be left in ignorance. And afterwards they'll say that nobody knew what Christ meant, that it won't be known down through the centuries."

OSCAR: "I think it also means we shouldn't be stupid, because we shouldn't let ourselves be robbed. But we're so stupid that we stand there with our arms crossed, and we pretend to be deaf, and we don't fight. We want a kingdom without a struggle. But there we have to struggle. That's violence. Knock down anybody that's screwing us, anybody that tries to rob us."

ESPERANZA: "But you can understand that only through the Gospel. Because think of all the people that are born with nothing, and so they say: 'What the hell can they steal from me, I've got nothing to steal.' And maybe they're working on a hacienda, and they don't even know they're getting robbed."

JULIO: "That's why you've got to have ears."

FELIPE: "And then there's guys that don't have shit and they say: 'Oh, communism! It takes everything you've got.'"

ESPERANZA: "You've got to have ears and understand what these Gospel words mean."

OLIVIA: "It seems we have a real responsibility to love. It's not just hearing, but, like Esperanza says, we've got to understand, too. We can't say afterwards: 'I didn't understand.' Jesus tells us we have that obligation, 'guys that have ears ought to listen.' Because if we don't we're not caring about others, and that's committing a crime."

I: "There are people here in Solentiname that don't even have ears, and they never come here to listen."

ESPERANZA: "That's why you have to understand. This isn't for everybody. You have to understand is what he means."

I: "And Jesus saw that they weren't listening to him. His words were having no effect. And that's why he goes on to say:

With what can I compare the people of these times?
They are like children who sit down to play in the parks
and they shout to their companions:
"We played the flute for you but you didn't dance.
We sang sad songs for you but you didn't weep."

I: "Jesus makes a very nice comparison: children who don't want to play anything. Their companions suggest that they play 'wedding,' but they don't want to. They suggest that they play 'funeral,' but they don't want to. Everything bores them. Maybe Jesus was remembering the games of his childhood.

People are like those children that won't get into the game. That's why there's no kingdom. And Jesus explains what those two kinds of games were:

> *Because John came, who neither ate or drank,*
> *and you say he has an evil spirit.*
> *Then came the Son of Man, who eats and drinks,*
> *and you say he is a glutton and a drunkard,*
> *a friend of sinners and tax collectors.*
> *But wisdom is shown in its works.*

OSCAR: "It's good to have Jesus say he drinks. If you didn't have fun, you'd really be screwed."

I: "There were two ways of presenting the kingdom, John's way and his way. John led a life of fasting and prayer, and they said he was possessed of the devil, which at that time was like saying he was crazy. Jesus led a normal life and even went to parties, but they rejected him just the same."

OSCAR: "The same thing happened to John and to Christ. They killed them both. And nowadays it's the same. You have to suffer. To be able to triumph you also have to die. But what good to us is a body that all it can do is move and not do anything useful. Jesus there was referring to the exploiters who didn't care a damned thing about other people.... Oh, I can't go on. My tongue's confused. Let somebody else talk. I'm a fool."

NATALIA: "John used to pray, maybe so people would accept the kingdom, but they didn't listen to him. He went on praying. They asked him if he was the Messiah, and he said: 'He'll be coming soon.' "

I: "The trouble is that John also spoke up against exploitation. He attacked Herod and the ruling classes. John was a great religious figure. He created a religious movement. But that didn't make them accept him, because he was a revolutionary. Without that, they would have accepted the long prayers and the fasting. And so if we had a Christianity with lots of religious devotions, but also revolutionary, they wouldn't accept it. And a Christianity without religious devotion or ritual, but revolutionary, they won't accept that from us either."

FELIPE: "I see one thing: the people have no reason to be afraid of revolutions. I can see why people who weren't poor were against John and Jesus, because neither of them talked in favor of the rich, just the opposite. They preached Christianity, the liberation of the poor."

I: "But I believe Jesus sees that he's ignored not only by the rich but also by the poor, who were influenced by the ideology of their leaders. Jesus here is talking about people in general, without distinction: 'What can I compare people of these times to?' "

ANTIDIO: "I wanted to say something about that, with regard to what Natalia said and what Felipe has just said: one of the biggest problems in any revolution isn't the rich at all; it's the poor people. They've taken everything away from the poor. And among the things they've taken away is the sense to understand their situation, or, using the Gospel words, they've taken away their ears. They've taken from them the knowledge that in them lies the force of the revolution. A very frequent problem among workers, laborers, and *campesinos* is that the poorer they are the less chance they have to realize that they're poor. When they take away from them everything that's the substance of living, they take from them even the sense of life. They can't understand anything because they've taken away even their understanding."

FELIPE: "They listen to the National Radio and they believe whatever they're told on it."

ANTIDIO: "They think like the rich, and that's their tragedy, because they're not rich. The rich have tricked the poor, making them think, feel, and react as if they were rich. The poor have no culture. What is meant by culture means in practice to be a complete human being. [I noticed that many people had tears in their eyes.] We can't be complete if we don't eat right, if we don't take care of our health, and if we don't get an education. People who don't eat right and don't take care of their bodies and can't get an education, they don't understand life. They don't know what life consists of. And they even believe they don't deserve it. The poor people that don't come here, I'd say, giving it a lot of thought, that it's not that they don't want to hear. The horrible thing is that they're not able to hear. It's only through a particular violent reality that they're able to hear. There are two kinds of poor people. The less poor are the ones that want to hear and can hear. They still have their ears, and they're the ones that help to make the revolution. The ones that can't hear, they never do hear, until the revolution comes and tells them: here's your food, here's your doctor, here's your school, here's your house, here's your job, here's your whole life. That's what happened in Cuba, as Ernesto tells in his book [*In Cuba* (New Directions, 1974)]. The ones that made the revolution were just a few people, helped by the bourgeoisie from the city and by a small part (though a very decisive and very important part) of the *campesinos*. But the revolution survives, not thanks to the ones that managed to make it succeed but to the ones that couldn't hear, but later, when the revolution came, they saw it and determined to defend it at all costs. And that's why there's a revolution. Fidel came down from the Sierra and made it succeed, with the help of the ones that had been able to hear. But Fidel has kept it going with people who hadn't helped him to make it; they heard only later when they saw it and they've been able to defend it: and that's the whole Cuban people. But the Cuban people didn't make the revolution; it was made by the part of the people that could hear. And the ones that couldn't hear because they didn't have ears, they got ears when the revolution won and they saw the deeds, they saw the reality. It was different from the reality that the rich, the ruling class, had told them was reality. They saw another reality, they joined the revolution, they became the revolution. So the revolution has two stages, the Cuban and any other one. It was begun first by the ones that could hear. Later it was kept going and made to grow by the ones that hadn't been able to hear because their ears had been taken away (and the revolution gave them back their ears, gave them back their awareness, their thought). And notice: they begin to think and be aware and hear from the moment when they eat, from the moment when they get taken care of. Because when people are eating right and don't have a bleeding mouth or their kids with stomachs and intestines all swollen, they have time to think. And when the people recover their thought, they realize that it's the people that make history, it's the people that do things and keep things going, it's the people that are the whole truth, which has been returned to them by the revolution. Then the people make the revolution grow, becoming part of it and prolonging it."

I: "And that is also a commentary on the last sentence that Jesus spoke: 'Wisdom is shown in its works.' Wisdom is the wisdom of God. Out of respect, Matthew doesn't mention the word 'God.' It's the plan that God has conceived with respect to the universe, or we might say it's the whole great cosmic process of evolution.

As for the 'works of God,' they have a very precise meaning in the Bible. They are God's works of liberation, ransoming his people from those who oppress them. Jesus also talks of the works of his Father, and he says that those are the works that he does, which is like saying that he is making his Father's revolution. They didn't accept John and they don't accept him, he says here, but wisdom, or God's cosmic plan, is shown through revolutionary action. We might say through its results. Not through words or ideology but through works. Antidio has already mentioned those works: food for everybody, medical services, education, etc. The good works that have been done in Cuba. These have been traditionally called works for charity, and we would better translate them as works of love."

I later said that we must also comment here on a passage of Luke in which he also talks of the kingdom of heaven and violence, but many think its meaning is different from Matthew's, and others think it's even opposed. Everyone agrees that it's also an obscure passage. It's Luke 16:16–17. Johnny, a boy of ten who is near me, offers to read it aloud. He stands up and reads:

> *Up until the time of John*
> *the law of Moses and the teaching of the*
> *   prophets were in effect.*
> *Since then the good news of the kingdom of*
> *   God has been proclaimed*
> *and everyone is struggling to get in.*

*It is easier for heaven and earth to cease to
    exist
than for a single letter of the law not to be
    fulfilled.*

I said that according to the Scripture scholars the meaning is also that all try to get in by
force, forcing their way in.

BOSCO: "The twenty centuries that have
passed since John are nothing compared with
the enormous number of centuries that humanity has had. And in these twenty centuries history has accelerated a lot, and is ac-
celerating more and more. And besides, we
now know which way history is going, and we
can begin to steer it ourselves."

FELIPE: "It seems to me that it used to be
that people understood the law of Moses and
the teaching of the prophets but they didn't
follow them; they were useless."

I: "The law was to love your neighbor like
yourself, and also that the people of Israel
ought to remain free, and that there should be
no slavery among them, and no poverty, and
this was also the teaching of the prophets. But
they couldn't put all this into practice, even
though the law and the teaching were very
clear, as Felipe says."

IVAN: " 'Since then the good news has been
proclaimed' means there's going to be a radical change. A new society's coming. It means a
lot."

NATALIA: "For me the good news is that
we're all going to be free."

I: "It's good news for the poor; if it's good for the poor it must be bad for the rich."

MYRIAM: "As I see it the ones that are struggling to get in are the ones that already want to change."

I: "But he says *all.*"

MYRIAM: "Maybe it's all the poor."

BOSCO: "Maybe there are some selfish bastards that are trying to get in."

JUAN, the seven-year-old son of Teresita and William: "To make people scared."

I: "To make people scared. For example, Pinochet and others like him. They also talk of creating a perfect society."

BOSCO: "It seems to me that all that about everybody struggling to get in will be when they're screwed, when they don't have their Miami anymore and they have nowhere to go. Everybody'll want to get into the revolution, when the revolution's world wide."

TERESITA: "Not everybody's going to get into the revolution."

I: "Here it only says that everybody *wants* to."

TERESITA: "Then, when there's no more Miami, I don't know what they're going to do."

BOSCO: "The way I figure it: when they don't have their Miami or anywhere to go, those bastards have got to get in or try to get in by force."

I: "What it says here is that ever since John the Baptist everyone has been trying or struggling to get in."

ELVIS: "Like Somoza saying his government is revolutionary."

JOHNNY, the ten-year old, in a soft voice: "I heard him."

JUAN, the seven-year-old, who is next to Johnny, in a loud voice: "Johnny says he heard him."

I: "I believe that here 'everyone' refers to revolutionaries and fascists. Jesus says that everyone wants to get in, not that everyone is going to get in. If they ask Pinochet if he wants a just society, he'll say yes, and that he's creating one, that he's establishing the kingdom of heaven." (Johnny, Juan, and other children with them think this is very funny.)

JUAN: "He's doing a lot of evil."

I: "Nevertheless he's doing a lot of evil, as Juan says. We've now understood this bit about everyone struggling, which seemed confused before. Afterwards Christ says that heaven and earth can cease to exist, but that not a single letter of the law will fail to be fulfilled. He really doesn't say 'letter' but something smaller, a tilde or a kind of accent over certain Hebrew letters."

BOSCO: "It seems to me it's like saying the laws of Marxism have to be fulfilled, and that history is going inevitably toward communism. It will be easier to destroy the earth than for those laws not to be fulfilled."

I: "And that's a lovely thought."

BOSCO: "That part's very encouraging."

ELVIS: "It's a process that can't be stopped. And Allende said a lovely thing: 'History is ours, and the people are making it.'"

I: "What Allende is saying is the same thing that Christ is saying. This is very beautiful, because the law of the Bible was the law of a perfect society. There are many who believe that there will never be on earth a society in which everyone loves one another, in which there is no injustice or selfishness, no grief or weeping, even though the Apocalypse says that all tears will be wiped away."

BOSCO: "Somoza has just said in a speech that there's got to be rich and poor, because if there's no rich who's going to help the poor? [The children laugh again.] And he said 'If nobody is the owner of the land, who is going to give work to the *campesinos*?' "

TERESITA: "It's through ignorance that they don't know where history is going. Poor people don't know that. In Cuba everybody studies Marxism, and they know the law has to be fulfilled; history always advances."

JUAN: "Without the rich the poor would live well."

I: "What Juan says is quite right, the opposite of what Somoza says. Somoza says the poor would be very badly off without the rich, but it's just the opposite, isn't it, Juan?"

ALEJANDRO: "I think that just as Antidio a while ago gave Cuba as an example, we can also give Solentiname. You all know that this group that meets here is criticized a lot by those who stay at home. They say that here there are no prayers, no saints. But they don't pray at home. Or that we smoke inside the church, or because after Mass we have a drink under the mango trees. They also drink (and get drunk) in their houses. And it's not that I want us to be praising ourselves, but I believe that good works are done here, works of wisdom, I could name a few, but there's no need."

ANTIDIO: "I'm in a position to say, because I'm from Venezuela, that this group that's commenting on the Gospel has an influence on other Christians and on other Marxists outside of Nicaragua. The ones that stay at home, the most they'll do is take a few drinks at home, and I don't think drinks at home are any holier than drinks in church. This group is influencing revolutionary thought (to speak only of what I know directly, but I could tell you much more) in the Christians and Marxists of Venezuela. This is true to such an extent that, for example, there's a very important Catholic in Venezuela and, when it was said there that Ernesto was having some problems in Nicaragua and that maybe he was going to decide to give up his work here, this guy said to me very seriously: 'Well, you tell Ernesto and his people in Solentiname, you write to them, that they don't belong just to Nicaragua, that they belong to us, too, that they must think of us, that thanks to them we've settled a series of things that were very serious and we've cleared up a lot of questions.' So the ones that stay home there, all they do is stay home and they can't make their voices heard or have an influence on the rest of the countries of America or on other countries in other parts of the world. Because you must know that what is said here is translated into several languages. What has come out of here

is very important. I insist again and I repeat:
there are Christians and Marxists that say
that what happens in Solentiname is like a
laboratory for America. I say this not so you'll
feel very important but so you'll feel very
much needed. I also want to say one thing
about the poor, to finish. The poor are (among
many other things that I could spend all morning listing) the workers, the ones who build the
roads, the highways, and the trucks, too. They
fish, they sow cotton, coffee, therefore they
are the *makers*: they make the roads, they
make the cotton, they make the coffee, they
make the trucks, they make everything.
Therefore they're the ones that make the
world. So we come to the following: they make
things, and once they make them (and they're
always making them), the things aren't for
them. They're taken away from them. Then
the poor are the ones that make the world but
they can't enjoy the world. The world is enjoyed by the ones that don't make it, the ruling
class, the rich. That's in the first place. In the
second place, as the poor are so busy working
and making things, they have no time to think.
They're poor, they own nothing, all they have
is *work*. That's all they have. They're animals
that get wages so they can recover the physical strength they used in working, so they can
go back to work the next day, the next week,
the next month, the next year. Or they're
like machines, like a boat motor that needs
gasoline or whatever you call it here to go on
functioning as a boat motor, but all its life it

will be just a boat motor. They go filling the laborer with gasoline, which is the few coins they give him for rice and beans and a tortilla, so he won't starve to death and go on being a useful object producing for others but not for himself. And a man that spends all day producing for others and eating and sleeping just to build up his strength and go on again just the same way the next day, a man like that, he can't think about what I've been saying, that he makes the world and that he's changing it. That's why history has needed Christ, Marx, people who aren't poor. They belong to the ruling class but they're traitors to it (and the word 'treason' sounds very well here). They're turncoats, that is, they abandon their class because they feel ashamed to belong to a ruling class. [I interrupted Antidio to tell him that Christ didn't belong to the ruling class.] No, he didn't but he was God, so I've put him in the same category. These people of the ruling class were aware that the poor make the world, that they're transforming it. They are the theoreticians, the intellectuals. Marx was no laborer. Engels was no laborer. They were aware that the wisdom of the world was produced by the poor. They took this wisdom and they wrote the books that are revolutionizing the world. That brings us to the following: It's necessary for the poor, for the workers of the world, to become conscious of what they are doing unconsciously. They are told this by those who abandon the ruling class. They tell them that they have a great culture. They tell

the poor: you're the ones that are making all
this, you're the owners of all this. We awaken
your consciousness, we give you back your
ears so you can rise up and take possession of
all that is yours and take away from the rich
what is not rightly theirs, and you recover it
not just for yourselves but for all of humanity.
The rich are a class that have decided that
they alone are all of humanity. Whereas now,
what is demanded of the poor and the workers
is that they work for humanity, and even for
the rich, because the rich are perhaps the
poorest of all. They're not even people, they're
nothing but *rich* people. So the poor have two
obligations: in the first place, instead of being
poor people, become people, recover all that's
been taken from them, and at the same time
take away from the rich what they have so
that the rich, once they've lost what they
have, can become people. So the work of the
revolution done by the workers consists of
making people of all of us who aren't people,
and none of us are, we're either poor or rich,
not people. And that's the great responsibility
of the working class, in the country or in the
city, people like you. It's not a question of per-
secuting the rich guy or even jailing him. We
have to be sorry for those poor guys; of course,
now's not the time to be sorry, that's for later.
Later we'll have to feed them and send them to
the hospital and educate them, re-educate
them."

NATALIA: "They've become rich through the
poor, because that's why they're rich, through

the poor, who've given them their riches."

ANTIDIO: "They're bandits, and every bandit, especially at that rank, is not a person. Being a person is something they don't know anything about."

ALEJANDRO: "Che's new human being. That's what a person is."

ANTIDIO: "And I repeat that those who live in Solentiname mustn't feel that they belong only to Solentiname or to Nicaragua. They also belong to Christian and non-Christian political leaders in Venezuela and beyond. In Venezuela there's finally come a union of Christians and Marxists, who deep down (and on the surface, too) want the same thing. And there's nothing now that can separate them. This is so true that what is said here in this church is important to the communists because they feel that this is their affair, too. So there's no need to be separated now. The only thing that separates people is that some are rich and others are poor, some are exploiters and others are exploited."

NATALIA: "We really think the same as them, and so we're united, you might say, to their words."

ANTIDIO: "Well, the importance of Solentiname consists of what is said here, which is very good, and this is not the opinion of people with fake culture, which means almost all professors (I'm a professor, so I know what I'm talking about; it's a fake culture, right?) and because besides, what's said here comes from reality itself. It's not something dreamed or thought, and it comes from people like you, working people who at the same time have had the opportunity to think."

I: "It's very important for the poor to comment on the Gospels, which were also written by poor people, by fishermen. The Gospels with comments by the rich are very different. It's like the Gospels that used to be preached here, a Gospel interpreted according to the ideology of the ruling class. It began by stating that there couldn't possibly be a kingdom of God on earth. The kingdom of heaven was going to be only in heaven. On earth there would always be injustice, always rich and poor. And therefore neither Christ nor John the Baptist came to do anything on earth, as far as transforming it goes. We must continue with the prophets, *talking* about the kingdom of God, but not *doing* anything about it."

ADAN: "That means that 'he came to die to save us.'"

I: "But without changing the world."

ANTIDIO: "And the truth is that the ruling class, the rich, not only allow people, but they like people to say things, even things against them, so they can appear to be generous. What they never allow (they kill you first) is to do things against them. That's serious. But there are words that are deeds, like the words that occur here in this church. It's showing the way. It's not talk, it's action. The fact that the Gospel has to be read another way, interpreted another way, and that that other way moves you to action, not to dream or be resigned, not like the reactionary Gospel that, when I was sixteen or seventeen, I heard preached by my parish priest in Las Palmas de Gran Canaria, producing interpretations like this one: mothers shouldn't let their daughters ride bicycles because that makes them expose their legs."

I: "And because the Gospel isn't intended for discussion but for action. Christ says that wisdom is shown by its works. The Gospel is shown by its works, doing what has been done in Cuba."

OLIVIA: "I'd say just as it's happening here in Solentiname. There are people who say there's nothing religious here, that Ernesto has nothing at all religious about him. Then I say to them: if you don't see the works."

OSCAR: "They're just bastards."

NATALIA: "Stupid people. You remember, Olivia, when this church was full of saints and nobody came, and that time there was going to be a Mass. We had to open a path with machetes, beginning at four in the morning, so people could get in, all thickets it was, and inside there were the saints, all filthy, covered with bat shit, and who came?"

OLIVIA: "It's the works, here we see the works that Christ talks about, love, and those who get liberated gradually see what the Gospel is like. But the others want none of that; they'd rather go away and not come back; they're poor people with the ears of rich people."

ALEJANDRO, her son: "It's because they

don't hear, says Antidio. They don't see or hear!"

I: "We have to make clear that here we're not yet doing the works of the Gospel. It's Olivia's goodness of heart that makes her say that the works are here. A few medicines that we give out don't mean a thing, and we really don't have many. And the fact that we're making known abroad the primitive paintings of the Solentiname *campesinos* is of little importance. We help in little ways. The works, homes, schools, hospitals, clinics: these can't be achieved by this little group gathered in this church."

ANTIDIO: "In a certain way, without exaggeration but also without denying it, this Mass and this Gospel commentary that's happening here is happening for thousands of people who aren't here. I don't know how many copies have been sold of the first volume of *The Gospel in Solentiname*, but I'll give you this fact: In Venezuela, when I came here, they had sold a thousand copies. That's a thousand people getting the message about what's being done here. It's a Mass that afterwards multiplies, like a seed that you sow and later it becomes many more. What's important about the sale of the book is not that the book is sold, or even that it's read. It's a book that's meant to be thought about. And the people that read this book are always people that want to do something. And the person that buys one of these books lends it to one or two other people. So that when we're here, and we're only sixty or seventy people, it's not really true that we're sixty or seventy. At this very moment, in a real way though not physically present here, we're five, six, seven thousand. [I interrupt Antidio to tell him that the copies that have been sold, in several languages, may be already thirty thousand.] Plus what's been published in newspapers and magazines and what's been read in college lecture rooms, where students ask you for copies. And it's not just other Christians who are interested in all this. Everyone is interested who, to say it evangelically, has good will, and 'will' means to want to do something. And what they want to do is, well, to build a new kind of society. And the interest and even the passion that this arouses, don't you believe it's just Christian feeling. It's rather the non-Christians who are eager to read these things. And I'm not the only one that can tell you this. Mayra can tell you too, for she moves in the same circles as I do. And I mention this simply as I told you before, so you'll feel not important but needed. Like other groups in other places. You must be aware that you're not alone or isolated. You're helping others. Just as others are helping you, for example, by buying Solentiname paintings. There are people who buy Solentiname paintings not only because they like the paintings, which are very beautiful, but also because they come from Solentiname. As I come from outside I talk to you this way. If I lived here maybe I wouldn't be talking this way, but as I come from outside I tell you what I bring from outside...."

Antidio went on talking, but our recording tape was used up on both sides.

24.

The Rich Epicure and Poor Lazarus

(Luke 16:19–31)

It's the parable of the rich man that had parties every day, while the poor man was at his door covered with sores.

FELIPE: "I think the poor man here stands for all the poor, and the rich man for all the rich. The poor man is saved and the rich man is damned. That's the story, a very simple one, that Jesus tells."

I: "Christians usually believe that the good rich man is saved and only the bad rich man is condemned. But that's not what is said here. The rich man isn't called evil, he's just called rich. And why is he damned?"

Little ADAN: "Because he was happy."

ELVIS: "While the other was screwed."

I said that was exactly what Abraham says in the parable, when the rich man in his place of torment asks for a drop of water:

> *My son, remember that you had things very*
> *good in your life,*
> *and Lazarus had them very bad.*
> *Now he is comforted here, and you suffer.*

FELIPE: "What I think is that neither the rich nor the poor ought to suffer the fate of those two guys in the Gospel. The rich man damned for having squandered selfishly, and the poor man screwed all his life even though afterwards he's saved. Which means there shouldn't be rich or poor, nobody should be screwed in this life, nobody should be damned in the next life. All people ought to share the riches in this life and share the glory in the next one."

ALEJO: "Yes, then the rich man couldn't have thrown parties every day; maybe he could have thrown parties, but not every day, and Lazarus could have been at those parties."

GLORIA: "The rich man's sin was that he had no compassion. Poverty was at his door and that didn't disturb him at his parties."

JULIO: "Now there are lots of Lazaruses that the rich have at the doors of their parties."

I: "And the poor man is badly off because the rich man is well off, or the rich man is well off because the poor man is badly off. There are poor people because there are rich people, and there are rich people because there are poor people. And rich people's parties are at the cost of the poor people."

WILLIAM: "I've been thinking what to do to

give an interpretation to this passage that
wouldn't be the one that's traditionally given
to it, and that seems to me wrong, and that has
been used for exploitation: because the poor
man has been led to believe that he must pa-
tiently endure because after death he's going
to be better off and that the rich will get their
punishment."

FELIPE: "As I see it, this passage was rather
to threaten the rich so they wouldn't go on
exploiting; but it seems it turned out the opposite: it served to pacify the people."

ALEJANDRO: "You don't want to see either of
them screwed. If we were selfish we'd say: let
the rich continue with their scheme and let the
poor man get saved. But that would be kind of
bad, wouldn't it? To want the rich man to get
screwed because of his wealth."

PANCHO: "This Gospel is for the rich, and
they ought to listen to it."

JULIO: "There's no point in its being for them
if they don't read it, and if they do read it they
pay no heed. The rich man of this parable cares
nothing for God; and that's the way the rich
still are nowadays."

OLIVIA: "I think the word of God has been
very badly preached, and the church is much
to blame in this. It's because the Gospel hasn't
been well preached that we have a society
still divided between rich and poor. There
are few places like this one where the Gospel
is preached and we understand it. Also, it's
us poor people who understand it. Unfortunately, the rich don't come to hear it. Where

the rich are, there's no preaching like that."

FELIPE: "But you know we can work to be rich too."

OLIVIA: "Nobody here works to get rich."

FELIPE: "Or at least to have more than the others, or to exploit others if we can."

MARIITA: "Or maybe at least we're not willing to share. Here the rich man's sin was not sharing. Not sharing with everybody, that is, with the poor, too; because he *did* share with the rich: the Gospel says he gave parties every day."

OLIVIA: "It was with other rich people like himself."

JULIO: "They weren't inviting the poor; they'd get their houses dirty."

OLIVIA: "And why didn't they preach this before, I want to know!"

MANUEL: "But all the rich go right on without believing, Doña Olivia, even though a dead man comes back to life."

We read that the rich man asked for the resurrection of the poor man so that he could go and convince the rich man's five brothers, who were also rich. And Abraham answered:

> *If they don't want to heed Moses and the
>   Prophets,*
> *they are not going to believe, even though a
>   dead man comes to life.*

I: "I believe this parable was not to console the poor but rather to threaten the rich; but as you said, William, it has had the opposite effect, because the rich weren't going to heed it. But Christ himself is saying that in this parable: that the rich pay no attention to the Bible."

LAUREANO: "In the churches in the big cities you see exactly the same picture that's painted here: inside are the bourgeois at Mass, and maybe outside in the courtyard there are some beggars."

I: "And surrounding the quarters of the rich are those miserable quarters covered with sores. Now in the bourgeoisie there is a Pentecostal Movement, which is above all lots of reading of the Bible, but they don't believe what Moses and the Prophets say, that is, the message of liberation in the Bible."

FELIPE: "Because for them it's like reading a bunch of nonsense that makes no sense."

OSCAR: "It seems like it doesn't do any good to be reading the Bible, then, because if you don't want to change the social order, you might as well be reading any damned thing, you might as well be reading any stupid book."

I: "It seems to me that Jesus' principal message is that the rich aren't going to be convinced even with the Bible, not even with a dead man coming to life (and not even with Jesus' resurrection)."

"So what can we do?"

ALEJANDRO (joking): "Force them to believe."

ELVIS: "The message is also, it seems to me, that humanity should not go on like that with those two classes: the one of the guy that throws parties every day, and the one of the guy that's at the door covered with sores."

WILLIAM: "Abraham has told the rich man who is being damned that there is an 'abyss' between him and the other man. There is an impassible, total separation. And it's the rich man who has placed that abyss of separation between the two of them."

I: "There are now advanced sectors among Christians who don't believe much in hell. It seems to me a very revolutionary dogma: that there is a place of damnation and that the rich are in it."

25.

The Expulsion of the Merchants from the Temple

(Matthew 21:12–17)

They came from Canada to make a film here. They wanted it to be a kind of message from Solentiname for the president-elect of the United States. They had no pre-conceived idea. The film would be what the people spontaneously would wish to say here. It would be entitled: *A Memorandum for Carter.* They began by filming the commentary on the Gospel of this Sunday.

> *Afterwards Jesus went into the temple and*
> *threw out all those who were selling and*
> *buying there.*
> *He overturned the tables of the money changers*
> *and the stands of the pigeon sellers;*
> *and he said to them:*
> *"In the Scriptures it says:*
> *'My house will be called a house of prayer,'*
> *but you have made it a den of thieves."*

257

While cameras are focusing on us from various angles:

OLIVIA: "I think he drove them out because they were exploiting people, because all trade is exploitation, and not because they were profaning the temple with cows and other animals. The desecration of the temple was the exploitation."

GLORIA: "And, as I see it, that action was against all those people that trade with religion."

WILLIAM: "And in general against all the people who have made use of religion (of the various religions down through history) to maintain a system of exploitation."

ESPERANZA: "The difference between the temples before and the temples now is that now there are no animals in the temples. But the traders are still inside."

ALEJANDRO: "They make no distinction between robbery and trade."

BOSCO: "Well, trade is appropriating the surplus-value of another; if not, it's not business."

I: "Apart from the Gospels there are documents that say that the trading concessions in the temple were in the hands of a few powerful families, among them the family of the high priest. It seems that Jesus' action wasn't so much against the merchants that he was driving out of there, and who were just employees, as it was against the highest authorities who were responsible for that organization. It's against them that the accusation of Jesus is directed, that they have converted the temple into a den of thieves. I have also read an interesting commentary: that the word 'thieves' in Greek means 'guerrilla fighters,' just as now the members of the Sandinistas are called criminals by the Military Court. They used to call the zealots thieves, and Jesus probably uses the word to tell the authorities that it's they who are the thieves and not the guerrilla fighters up in the mountains."

OSCAR: "The temple ought to be a place of unity (where God would be present among them), and if there was exploitation it wasn't a place of unity anymore. Because that trading was against love, and God couldn't be there anymore."

I: "We have to keep in mind that the money changers were needed for the offerings that had to be made with a special kind of coin, the ancient temple coin, because they didn't allow there the current money, which was Roman. And the sale of the animals was for the sacrifices. The Gospel mentions only the pigeons, perhaps because that was the commonest sacrifice since it was the sacrifice of the poor people (Mary, as a poor woman, offered one of those pigeons when Jesus was born). So that commerce performed a liturgical function. But it seems that Jesus didn't care much about the worship; what he cared about was stopping the trading."

FELIPE: "When in a country like Cuba there

are no more merchants, and they don't even allow street hawkers, the temple has been purified."

I: "Jesus joins in a single phrase two quotations from the prophets: one is from Isaiah, in which God says that his house will be called a house of prayer for all the peoples, and another from Jeremiah, in which he says that they have converted his house into a den where thieves gather. That business about its being a house of prayer isn't the most important thing here for Jesus but that it should be *for all the peoples*. And the contradiction that he sees isn't so much between prayer and trading; the irreconcilable contradiction is that the house of prayer that ought to be to unite all the people and to free all of humanity has been converted into a center for the exploitation of the people and a business place for a few."

ALEJANDRO: "Here all trading is condemned, not just trading inside churches. All trading is crap. Because he doesn't tell them: You've made the temple into a trading center. He tells them: You've made it a den of thieves."

WILLIAM: "Selling isn't bad, the way it's done in Cuba. It's lending a service. As long as it isn't done for profit."

I: "Like the people that come to sell bread or soda on Sundays; and we let them sell right here inside the church. For example, there's Doña Felipa with her breadbasket, and she's going to sell bread after Mass inside the church, and none of us see that as a desecration."

ALEJANDRO: "There are times when some people slip up. Sure, naturally they have to make their little profit, get the best of the other guy; there's no reason to lend a service for nothing, and we're in a system where we have to live with this kind of thing; but don't let them go too far."

NATALIA: "Any trading that's done without charity, that's what's bad."

I: "When I was in Chile, a revolutionary monk who belonged to MIR told me that it was very clear that this had been a commando action. Jesus by himself couldn't have overturned the tables with the money and the booths and driven out all the merchants. It's known that there was a temple policeman who kept order."

OLIVIA: "It's possible. I hadn't understood it that way, but it's possible."

I: "He went in with a lot of people. The Gospel says afterwards that the authorities didn't dare to proceed against him because of fear of the people. They probably went in through the various doors of the temple, and it was a surprise action. Matthew says he threw out not only the sellers but also those who were buying, and John adds that he forbade them to go around inside the temple carrying loads, so the control of the temple was complete. And as if that wasn't enough, he afterwards began to teach in the temple. The Gospel relates the triumphal entry of Jesus into Jerusalem the

day before. He had entered like a king. There
existed the custom of laying red carpets as
kings passed, and when the crowds spread
their cloaks before him it meant that they
were proclaiming him king. Matthew says
that at that entrance 'the whole city was much
moved.' And Mark adds a significant detail,
that Jesus, after his triumphal entry into
Jerusalem, *inspected* the temple. He said he
reached the temple, 'and after looking all
around at things, he went off to Bethany with
the twelve disciples because it was getting
late.' "

ALEJANDRO: "It was like the seizing of
churches that's been going on everywhere."

GLORIA: "And the Romans let him do that?"

I: "The Romans were much concerned about
the temple, because it was the center of the
Jews' political power. Above it there was a
Roman tower, the Antonia Tower, from where
the soldiers were always spying on the temple.
The seizure of the temple occurred in sight of
the Romans. They let it take place considering
that it was an internal struggle of the Jews."

WILLIAM: "Just as the U.S. intervention in
our countries doesn't meddle in partisan
struggles, when they think those struggles
don't threaten their interests, and that instead those internal divisions favor their interests."

I: "Pilate cared nothing about Jesus' messianism, because he considered it a religious
conflict, until the Jewish authorities made
him see that the messianism had serious polit-

ical implications, that it meant that Jesus was king, and that the very power of Rome was being threatened. And Jesus didn't deny this to Pilate. He didn't say: I'm not coming to meddle in politics. He told him: I am king, and that's why I came into the world."

WILLIAM: "It was a symbolic action that he performed. Because the following day merchants were going to be right back again. It seems to me he wasn't interested in purifying that temple of Jerusalem; his action was projected toward the future."

I: "The text of Isaiah that Jesus quotes doesn't say 'My house *is*' but 'My house *will be* a house of prayer for all peoples'; he was referring to the messianic era. So, as William says, Jesus wasn't trying to purify the temple of the Jewish religion (a temple that instead he was coming to destroy) but he was performing a symbolic action to show that with it the messianic era was already beginning, and that the new temple of the messianic era was already being inaugurated, the temple that would be for all peoples, and in which there could no longer be thieves. And Jesus was surely alluding to another prophecy, of Zacharias, that says: 'There will be no more merchants in the house of the Lord on that day.'"

JULIO: "It seems to me he wasn't referring to the temple, the temple like this one. He was referring to a person's temple. That a person is a temple. That's why no person should do evil business, it seems to me."

I: "That's why we say it was a symbolic ac-

tion. Afterwards the first Christians understood that they must not worship in temple.
Saint Paul tells how he was praying in the
Jerusalem temple and there he had a vision in
which he was told to get out of there. Saint
John in the Apocalypse says that in the New
Jerusalem there will be no temple (it would
seem that it's an atheistic materialistic Marxist that is talking), and he adds that the temple
will be the whole universe. He means that
there must not be any business deals, not only
in church alcoves but also in the streets, in the
squares, or in commercial centers; there must
be no exploitation in the whole universe."

WILLIAM: "Julio calls evil business what
businessmen call good business."

There in the temple some blind men and
*   cripples approached and he cured them.*
But when the chief priests and the teachers of
*   the law saw the miracles that he was per-*
*   forming,*
and when they heard how the children were
*   shouting in the temple:*
"Hosanna to the Son of King David!"
they said to him:
"Do you hear what they are saying?"

I: "'Hosanna' is a Hebrew word that is
equivalent to 'Hurray,' and it literally means
'Free us, then!' It was a shout of acclaim
for a leader. They are shouting: Hurray for
King Jesus! The Gospel says that the children

were shouting: I think it's referring to the young people. They were probably the young people that went in with him on that commando operation. They probably weren't young kids who would have had no reason to be doing such a thing."

ALEJANDRO: "They were like, say, students."

I: "The Gospel has said that it was with that shout of 'Hosanna' that they had greeted him the day before in Jerusalem. It was probably those same 'children,' the young people, who were the principal ones to acclaim him as king."

ALEJANDRO: "Yes, when he says the children they must be them, the young people. Because it used to be that young people between fifteen and eighteen weren't worth much; it was the old people who bossed everything, and those old people must have been great reactionaries."

WILLIAM: "In those times the leaders were called ancients, because only the old had any authority. That's why the first Christians called their leaders 'presbyters,' which means ancients, even though they were young."

ALEJANDRO: "The young people were with him. And that made the leaders really mad."

I: "What the kids were shouting made them mad. And it seems that Jesus answered them joking, to make them even madder, quoting a Psalm from the Bible."

*Yes, I hear them. But haven't you read the
scripture that says:
"Out of the mouths of children and infants
you receive perfect praise"?*

JULIO: "I see young people shouting now as
they shouted when they were with Jesus in the
temple. The young people now want a change
too, and this shouting is not pleasing to the
rich, the ones who are enjoying their privileges, and so they try to shut them up. They
really don't want to hear the young people
shouting 'Hurray for change! Hurray for joy!'
Because what they want is to have oppression
and sadness."

I: "Even though those old men didn't want to
hear those voices, these young people had
burst out into the streets of Jerusalem, when
Jesus entered, shouting 'Hurray for the revolution!' That means exactly the same as the
Gospel sentence: 'Blessed be the kingdom to
come!' The word 'kingdom' on the lips of Jesus
meant the same as the word 'revolution' now
means."

JULIO: "And that's why they killed him. And
they'll go right on killing anyone that wants a
change, a new kingdom, a revolution."

WILLIAM: "He must have gone into the temple with his people. If he'd gone in alone they'd
have murdered him, because traders are the
worst people there are. And the people helped
him to overturn tables. It's clear that everything was well organized. And afterwards
there was a meeting. That reference here to

the blind and crippled means the temple was full of poor people."

I: "In addition to the young people, the students, who are the ones that shouted 'Hurray.'"

GLORIA: "But afterwards he came out. He didn't try to hold on to the temple."

WILLIAM: "If he had tried to, the Roman Marines would have arrived."

I: "He enters Jerusalem with the acclaim of the whole people. After the action in the temple he retires to Bethany where it seems he was in hiding. From then on he appears in public only by surprise. He finally goes into hiding, and to capture him they have to resort to the treachery of Judas. Afterwards, he was taken to the Sanhedrin where the temple business came up. He was accused through false witnesses of having said he would destroy 'this temple made by man's hands,' in order to build another one. But the phrase 'made by man's hands' may have been an authentic phrase of Jesus' and he probably said it to remind the Jews that that sacred temple had been built by Herod."

FELIPE: "After he drove out the traders Jesus taught in the temple. He was probably conscientizing them. He was probably teaching Christianity and talking against the temple."

LAUREANO: "Now the big churches are full of rich people, people from the Bank of America and from all the big banks, and the priests are preaching to them. But I don't think their preaching is worth a damn."

FELIPE: "He taught above all by example, driving out the traders and bankers, teaching us that we had to put an end to the exploitation of people by people. Even if it has to be done with a whip."

Someone asked, smiling: "With a whip, but not with a machine gun?"

FELIPE: "Either with a whip or a machine gun."

ALEJO: "Whichever is needed. Because the exploitation that capitalism makes of our bodies is a greater desecration than the one in the temple."

I: "The supporters of absolute nonviolence have a lot of difficulty explaining this passage. Some say that Christ here did not act like a man but like God, and that he could do those things as God. Others say that a whip was a gentle weapon that injures nobody. Others say that he wouldn't use the whip against men but only against animals, because in Greek it's not very clear whether he used the whip against men or against animals. None of that seems to me convincing. But in another commentary on the Gospel I read recently an interesting detail: that it was forbidden to enter the temple with weapons or clubs. Therefore the only weapon that Jesus could use was the one he used. The Gospel according to Saint John says that he took ropes and with them made a whip. It's more logical to think that they made many whips."

ESPERANZA: "And the fact that Jesus cured

the sick reminds me of Che, who in the midst of the attacks, when he was fighting, took care of people, because he was a doctor."

OLIVIA: "Che and others like him are like Christ, they seem a lot like Christ, and they are the ones that are purifying the temple of the traders and exploiters."

I: "The temple that is now the universe."

Before the dialogue ended something went wrong with the camera and they stopped filming. They couldn't fix the camera and the people who came to make the film had to return to Canada, leaving the project pending until another occasion.

26.

The Wedding Feast

(Matthew 22:1–14)

*The kingdom of heaven is like a king
who arranged a feast for the wedding of his
son.
He sent his servants to call those who had
been invited, but they would not come.*

OLIVIA: "Jesus compares the kingdom of God with a wedding feast, first, because that kingdom is a love like the love of two people that join in matrimony, and second, because the wedding feast is the most joyful of feasts, and that kingdom is a great joy, a great feast."

MANUEL: "Christ is the son; and our union with him is like the union of a couple."

FELIPE: "I think this ought to be cleared up a little: the truth is that when you join Christ is when you join the others, the comrades. To be joined to Christ without being joined to the others isn't possible. To be joined to the rest is to be joined to Christ."

I: "When we join the rest, we join Christ, and

since Christ is God we join God, and this union is like that of two spouses."

ALEJANDRO: "And the feast? Why do they say that the kingdom of God is a joy, a feast?"

I: "If there's a marriage between God and us, there has to be a celebration of that union, a feast."

ALEJANDRO: "But wouldn't love be like a continuous feast?"

I: "The true feast is the feast of love. This means this image that Jesus uses, of a feast with joy, music, dancing, liquor, a feast to celebrate a union of love."

Another: "The society that Jesus wants for us is a society of much joy."

ELVIS: "Probably he wants to have this society here on earth; and it will be a tremendous joy for all of humanity."

Another: "And the feast is also a gathering, right? The feast, to be really a feast, has to be with lots of people. Just four people gathered there don't make a feast."

WILLIAM: "The reason for the joy is that there are two who are getting married, who love each other."

OLIVIA: "And at the feast there's always a great abundance of good things. It seems like he's talking there about a society where there'll be a great abundance and it'll be shared. The kingdom of God isn't on earth yet because the meal isn't shared yet. It's love that's going to cause that sharing on earth, right? Because the cause of that feast was a wedding."

But the guests did not heed him.
One of them went to his estates, another to
his affairs.

LAUREANO: "Those were the rich. People that were in business, and people with lots of property; all they think about is their affairs, their property."

BOSCO: "The feast was very good. He had killed lots of steers and lots of pigs. He was inviting them sincerely. He was inviting them to have a good time. If they don't go, screw them. They turned down a good time to attend to their businesses."

OLIVIA: "The ones that defend their private interests, it seems to me they're the ones that don't get into the kingdom."

And others seized the king's servants
and they beat them and killed them.
Then the king was very angry
and he sent his soldiers to kill those murder-
ers
and to burn their town.

"But why were those guys so much against him?"

"They must have been from a city that was an enemy of the king, and they were against the wedding, and instead of going to the feast, what they want to do is make war on the king."

"Those are murderers. The rich aren't interested in the feast, and they simply don't go. And they don't want to have a feast, and they

kill the ones who are invited. Like today
there's people that persecute and torture and
kill people who are trying to do them good:
people who are inviting them to the feast of
love."

"The kingdom of heaven hasn't been established yet. It's a kingdom we're being invited
to. And we haven't yet seen that punishment
of the king who ordered that enemy city to be
burned down, where there must surely have
been another king. Or maybe we're seeing it
only in part. But one thing is certain: the feast
is not going to get ruined."

Then he said to his servants:
"All is ready for the feast,
but those guests did not deserve to come.
Go out then to the main streets
and invite to the wedding everybody you
  meet."

"It seems to me that this verse refers to the
simple class, to poor people like us."

"And those people that were hungry would
go running to the feast."

"I think this Gospel is very peculiar."

I: "It's certainly a very peculiar Gospel, and
we might say that Jesus is giving us an extravagant example: a king who gives a feast
and none of his guests arrive, and then he fills
the house with strangers from the streets.
Saint Luke says he sent out to invite the poor,
the lame, the crippled, and the blind, and afterwards he sent out to bring others by force to

the feast. We may say that this feast of the kingdom is also, from a worldly point of view, an extravagant feast: It's a great joy but it's not for those who have wealth and power but for the poor of the earth and for the underdogs."

"And some people will have to be ordered to go to that joy."

"I don't see why they had to invite the rich and the powerful first."

I: "It seems that Jesus saw that the rulers of society, the people with lands or businesses or power of any kind, were the ones who were called on to change society, but they didn't accept the invitation of history. The second invitation is for the ones on the sidelines, and they really came piling in."

LAUREANO: "Those were the ones that needed the sharing of the wealth. The rich didn't need any sharing."

FELIPE: "They went out to tell them that there's a very good meal, that there's a joyful feast, but those people have their own amusements or their own businesses and they're not interested in going to the feast. On the other hand, poor people are told that the king invites them to a great feast, that there's a heap of beef cooked there, and everybody goes."

"Even though it was only tamales."

FELIPE: "The same thing happens now. If you say to people that are well off that God has prepared a kingdom of abundance and love and joy for humanity, they're not much in-

terested. But if they're poor people, then they
are interested, and they're capable of struggling for that."

ALEJANDRO: "Others commit murder because the feast makes them mad."

I: "Jesus was probably seeing that his fol-
lowers were only poor people, and that the rich
and the powerful weren't interested in his
message, or were against it. And then he
thinks of this comparison. Humanity is divided in two, those who accept the invitation
to love and those who reject it; and this division corresponds to two social classes."

The servants went out into the streets and
gathered everyone they found, good and
bad;
and so the hall filled with people.

FELIPE: "The bad ones are going to get to
be good, the ones they call bad, people who are
going to change, and they'll also form the future society."

I: "The Pharisees thought they were the
good ones, and they thought the kingdom
would be a religious kingdom, of people who
were good according to them (religious people), and Jesus is saying that the kingdom will
be with all the poor on earth, good and evil, for
even among the poor there can be evil ones."

LAUREANO: "As a result of living in a corrupt society. People go around the streets robbing other people, and they do it because they
need to."

ALEJANDRO: "The important thing here is that Jesus is talking about all classes. It was only one class that arrived, the other didn't even come near. So the kingdom of heaven is identified with the poor, with that social class."

We read that later the king went in and saw one who was not wearing wedding clothes.

> *And he said to him:*
> *"Friend, how is it that you came in here*
> *without wedding clothes?"*
> *But the other one was silent.*
> *Then the king said to those who were waiting*
> *on table:*
> *"Tie him hand and foot and throw him into*
> *outer darkness,*
> *where he will weep and gnash his teeth."*

LAUREANO: "I'm sorry for the one they threw out because he was poorly dressed: he was probably going around all shitty."

I said that we may suppose that the king would have given a tunic to each guest.

"That one who was poorly dressed was just the same as the ones who wouldn't attend, the first ones invited. He too snubbed the king when he didn't accept the clothes; he came there just to make trouble and the king got sore, too."

"There are some who eliminate themselves, and those appear here as the rich. Among those who go in, there can be one who also scorns the feast, and that one has to be eliminated too."

DONALD: "And that one, wouldn't he be there to spy on the others?"

A recently arrived schoolteacher broke in, and we suspected that he could be a new spy that they've sent us, and he said a few incoherent phrases.

FELIPE: "That one arrived to join the party but he wasn't with the spirit of the feast, he wasn't sharing in the joy, and that's why he didn't want to put on that garment. Jesus wants us to see that among those who reach the kingdom there may be some who aren't worthy and they'll have to be thrown out."

"Man, look, I think we're having this meeting and we're talking here about the revolution, about love (for me, love is the revolution), and that we ought to unite, and maybe there's some shit that's listening, snooping on what we're talking about, our plan, and that bastard goes to the authorities and we find out he's a spy (that occurs to me because they've just said that man of the parable could be a spy) and then we'd get rid of him quick, because the group's not going to get screwed on account of him. Maybe the same thing happened at that wedding. That's why the king got sore and condemned him."

ALEJANDRO: "Maybe they questioned him and he couldn't answer."

For many are called, but few are chosen.

TERE: "And it's up to us to be chosen or to be rejected from the community. Jesus calls damnation the 'outer darkness.' It's being separated from the rest of the people."

I: "You don't go into hell, you come out into it. Hell, according to Jesus, is outside."

"And he's saying that, though the feast is for everyone, there's a bunch of people that don't accept it. That's why the kingdom takes time; everything is ready now, but there's had to be a second invitation."

OLIVIA: "Long ago, the kingdom of heaven would have been established, but through thinking about the God in heaven we haven't been concerned about the gods that suffer on earth."

ESPERANZA, who is going to marry Bosco soon: "I think this Gospel is very good. And very clear also."

I: "When I was in Chile, at the little hotel where I was staying, a monk came to see me who belonged to the M.I.R. (and he was armed and half underground, although it was during the government of the Popular Front), and he told me this parable: 'Humanity is now like a girl of twelve who doesn't want to play with dolls anymore, and she wants to be independent of papa and mamma; this is the atheism that all humanity is coming to, and it's positive because it's due to a process of maturing; religion belonged to the childhood of humanity. But the girl is not wholly mature; later she'll be a woman, and she'll feel alone and that she needs someone, and then God the bridegroom will appear. Right now she doesn't feel the need for marriage and we mustn't talk to her much about it so as not to upset her, but at times we have to talk to her a little so she won't grow up selfish or become a lesbian or try to commit suicide. The role of the contemplative monk is to remind that girl that she is destined to be wed. That wedding of God and humanity took place in the person of Jesus of Nazareth, but later it's going to take place with us all when we, all together, form a united humanity and we are all Christ. We are all cells of that body that is going to have sexual union with God.'"

"Now nobody's going to be a bachelor, and there won't be any loneliness anymore," said a bachelor.

OSCAR: "But let's not let happen to us what happened to that one: that we're put up against the wall."

27.

The Tribute to Caesar

(Matthew 22:15–22)

The Pharisees and Herodians joined forces to lay a trap for Jesus, asking him about the tribute to Caesar.

I: "The Pharisees and the Herodians were enemies, but they joined forces against Jesus. Herod was a defeatist; in his court they spoke the language of Rome, they dressed in Roman style, their customs and their festivals were Roman. The Pharisees were nationalists, but they were reactionaries, and in the long run they became reconciled with the Romans. If Jesus came out in favor of the duty, they would accuse him before the people as a collaborationist; if he came out as opposed to it, they would accuse him before the Romans as a subversive."

Jesus asked them to show him a coin and they showed him a denarius.

Jesus asked them:
"Whose is this face and the name that is written on it?"

280

They answered him: "Caesar's."
Then Jesus said to them:
"Then give to Caesar
what belongs to Caesar,
and to God what belongs to God."
When they heard this they were astonished;
and they left him and they went away.

LAUREANO: "What he did was confuse them. He confused them there; they probably didn't understand him, and that's why they went away."

I: "What Laureano says is quite true. He had to get away. He couldn't speak out, because if he did he'd fall into the trap. For a long time they've interpreted this in a reactionary way, that you have to serve the state, even though it's unjust, and God at the same time, giving to each one its own—as if Christ here ought to have talked clearly, when he's talking enigmatically. If Jesus had said simply that it was necessary to submit to Rome, he would have fallen into the trap, and that is what they wanted. In his story Luke adds that 'they could not accuse him before the people because of his words.' But the reactionaries go on making us believe that Jesus fell into the trap."

"I get the impression that he says that first we have to build the kingdom of love, and that the confrontation with Rome will come later. He didn't want to open a front on which he couldn't fight immediately, but he would leave it for later."

"And he points out to them a real fact.

When he asked them to show him a coin, they show him a denarius, which was the Roman coin."

"The dollar."

I: "It wasn't that the coins belonged to the emperor, they belonged to the empire. They had to admit that they were a colony, and this was a reality that couldn't be changed. The zealots, the supporters of armed struggle, thought they could struggle against Rome with swords, but that was suicide. And we also have to take into account that for Jesus the greatest oppression wasn't that of Rome but of the Jewish religious castes. The power of Rome could end, as in fact it did, and the oppressions continue. After the system of slavery, feudalism had to come, and afterwards, capitalism."

LAUREANO: "He's presenting communism as a goal, but you couldn't skip steps."

"As the emperor was fond of money, it seems to me, he even had his face portrayed on the coin. And that was like wanting all the money to belong to him. And then Jesus says that if he loved riches so much and wanted the riches of others to belong also to him, well, for the moment they had to leave him in his riches, that is, in his selfishness. And the idea that we must give to God what belongs to God means that we must give him what he asks of us, which is unselfishness and love."

LAUREANO: "Yes, it seems to me that what he's saying here is that we must give God love. To give God what belongs to God is to give him love, brotherly love, because love belongs to God since God is love. And that we should give our selfishness to the emperor, because money is selfishness. Because the emperor wants the money not for the poor but for himself and he doesn't want it to be distributed."

"It seems to me that he adds the business about God, counterposing it to the first, and in opposition to it. The business about the duty is a question of detail; they had to admit that they were a colony of the empire, but they had to attack the imperialist system when they gave to God what is God's, because God means liberation."

"It isn't that the money belonged to the emperor; the money belonged to the people, but he tells them to notice the coin, so they can see what imperialism is: a coin with the face of the man there. He wanted them to see that from the time when an emperor puts his name and face on a coin he's making himself boss of everything in the country, of everybody, of the money that belongs to everybody. And Jesus is showing them that Caesar's a complete dictator because he's putting his portrait on the coin and taking for himself what belongs to the people. He's telling them that he's grabbing the money, because he's pictured there as owner and lord of everything; then he wants to make himself owner even of the people, because he was on the money with which people were buying. Let's say that it's like now in Nicaragua, with Somoza, because Somoza is on the money, and we're all used to seeing him as the owner of Nicaragua; that's the way it was at that time. I believe he wants to tell them that all things belong to God, but that the emperor wants to make himself owner of everything when he makes himself owner of the people's money."

ALEJANDRO: "A businessman, a banker, are people that talk only about money, are portrayed on money, are money pure and simple. And that God, there, was something very different from money, was class struggle, struggle for a change, for the triumph of the people. He's telling them: that stuff about the emperor was only a question of money, but God is something different, with which we're going to defeat the dictator, the emperor; I believe that's the distinction that he's making, that God is more, that it's not just money but the whole economy."

I said that what Alejandro said was very true. Here Christ is making a distinction between God and money; and he's also making a distinction between God and the emperor. At that time the emperor was God. And the cult of the emperor was changing into a dominant religion in the whole empire. We have coins of Tiberius, emperor at the time of Christ, that say: "Tiberius, Caesar, son of the divine Augustus." That's just what was being said on that coin they took out. And Christ told them that the duty was one thing and worship was another. And he's also making a distinction between the kingdom of God and the Jewish nation. The zealots believed that just by freeing themselves from Roman control the

kingdom of God would be established. And
they thought that tribute was a sin because
those who were of the "people of God" could
not pay tribute to the pagans. The question
they ask him is of a moral nature: if it is *licit* to
pay tribute. And Christ is also answering for
the zealots. Besides I've read that the Greek
word that Christ uses means exactly "return."
So the phrase allowed another meaning: return that foreign coin that doesn't belong to
you. Anyway they understood that Christ was
not in favor of the duty, and that's why Luke
says that they couldn't accuse him "before the
people." And later they accused him before
Pilate of inciting the people not to pay the duty
to Rome.

"Because they knew that his doctrine was
against the imperialism of that time. And
against all imperialism. But the bastards laid
a good trap for him!"

"He gives them an answer like you can give
to a spy. From the beginning he calls them
hypocrites. He doesn't answer them as you'd
answer a man of good faith who wants to know
the truth. It's as if a spy came now to question
us and then to go to denounce us. He insults
them from the beginning, and in public besides."

I: "Of course Luke, in relating this passage,
adds the fact that those who came to Jesus
were 'spies.' "

"He acted like a politician, like a director of
the masses who's not letting himself be
screwed. He acted tactically."

"Besides he's dealing not only with the problem of the Jews; he's talking for all peoples."

"Yes, because they were thinking only about their local problem, to free themselves from the Roman Empire, and the rest of the earth was not liberated."

I: "Nor were they liberated from their other oppressions. Internal oppression, class oppression, that was worse. Because often local governments were worse than the government of Rome. The Roman Empire was more modern; it represented progress in comparison with other regimes of antiquity. Now we have overcome the stage of the emperor of the slave society, and that of the kings of feudal society, and we're overcoming that of capitalism. The day will come when it won't be necessary to give any tax to the state, and there won't be a state any more, and we're only going to give to God what belongs to God."

"The emperor no longer exists. But there's imperialism."

"Imperialism, then as now, has always been united with the money god."

"To give to God what belongs to God is to bring about revolution."

I: "Yes, because in the Bible God always reveals himself as Liberation. Yahweh is a force that impels us to change to revolution, that's the message of all the prophets. Here Christ is saying that we must give to God what belongs to God, and in another passage he says, repeating the Prophet Hosea, what it is that God wants us to give him: 'I want love and not sacrifices' (and not religious worship)."

WILLIAM: "But money isn't bad, it's good. It's the only thing that, because it's good, ought to belong to everybody. Money isn't selfishness. But money is to be circulated and selfishness consists of hoarding the money and preventing it from circulating."

I: "That's also very good what William says. We can sum this all up by saying that love consists of sharing the money, and giving to God what belongs to God is making people love one another and making the wealth belong to everyone. And in the end there'll be no more need for money. Isn't that right?"

"That's it."

At this Mass we had brother John with us. He was a young American visiting us. He wore sandals and a white robe with gold embroidery. His delicate profile, his parted beard, and his curly hair that came down to his shoulders gave him a close resemblance to Christ, as Christ is pictured in religious prints. He had been going around the world for six years, living only by begging alms, although his parents owned a luxurious hotel in South Africa. We noticed that wild dogs, as soon as they saw him, stopped barking and ran eagerly toward him; and babies gave great demonstrations of joy on seeing him. We were also very aware that his white robe was always immaculate, even though he had only one and slept in it in the streets or the fields. His belongings were minimal: a change of underclothes, one book (the Gospels), and a flute. He spoke Spanish very well.

JOHN said: "Dear brothers and sisters: I am brother John, a disciple of Jesus and a follower of Saint Francis of Assisi. I have been delighted to hear all that has been said here about the state and money. I want to add that Jesus asked them to show him a coin because he didn't go around with coins and he never touched money. Saint Francis didn't touch money either, and he forbade the Franciscans to touch it. I have tried to follow this example, and I go through all countries without using money. I'm not a hippy, although I was one. Through drugs I was converted to a life of meditation, chastity, and poverty, but for six years now I haven't used drugs. During the first two years I made a vow to live on charity without begging for alms, just waiting until someone gave me something; that was more difficult, sometimes I was afraid, but not once in the two years was I hungry. Now I feel freer and I can beg for alms; but I never beg for money and when I get more than I need at that moment I give it away at once. Living off other people is very good for you because you always have to be smiling and be very pleasant; if you aren't they won't give you anything. I get on a bus and I smile at the driver and I say to him: 'Dear brother, I am brother John, a disciple of Jesus, and I have made a vow not to carry money.' Almost always the driver sits me beside him and begins to ask me questions and I leave with him the message of love. If we get to a bridge and I see a river that I like, I ask him to stop and I get off right there and I bathe in that river. Then I find someone else who will take me where I was going. This way I've been traveling around Latin America. In Colombia another American pilgrim told me that he had heard of this community and I decided to come to Solentiname. In Cartagena I begged in the stores for ship passage to San Andrés Island, explaining that I wanted to go to Solentiname. In San Andrés the bishop took up a collection to buy me an air ticket to Managua. In Managua a beggar that I met in the cathedral offered to serve as my guide and showed me the whole city. The venders in the market offered me food the moment they saw me. The driver of a bus that was going to Granada invited me to get on without my asking him. In Granada a priest saw me in the park and took me to a home to sleep. When I arrived the lights were out; in the morning, when I woke up I realized that the house was full of old people. That made me very happy. I went to the dock and asked a boat to let me on board free because I wanted to go to Solentiname. In San Carlos sister Olivia saw me in the street and gave me food and led me to a boat that was coming to Solentiname, telling them not to charge me. From here I'll go to Costa Rica, where I know I'll find a boat that will take me to India, and I know that the boat will be a sailing ship. I used to be a university student, I was getting a degree in engineering, I dressed very well. I had money, and I was self-centered. One day I decided to follow the example of Saint Francis. At first I went around dressed as a Franciscan but at the Mexican border the Mexican Franciscans had the police arrest me because I wasn't a Franciscan. They were right, and since then I haven't worn the Franciscan habit, but I am a follower of Saint Francis, and they are not. In my wanderings I've been in jail several times but I'm never in very long because as soon as I'm jailed I stop eating and they have to let me out. I can't be imprisoned because I get very sad and I can only live free as the birds. I'd like to visit Cuba, but I don't know if they would let me beg there; there everything's controlled by a ration ticket. But I believe that in socialist countries they ought to allow beggars. At times I have doubts and I wonder if I'm not a parasite on society. But afterwards I think not, that I'm doing something useful, carrying a message around the world, with no need to preach anything: just seeing me. Maybe this type of life isn't suitable for a revolutionary country like Cuba; it's more suitable for a post-revolutionary world. For the present, we beggars announce that new world in which man can lead a life in a brotherly way and free and without money. That's why I go around disguised with this costume (I'm aware that this is a disguise). I go around like a clown, to attract attention, and so they'll give me alms, for they wouldn't give to me if they saw me in ordinary clothes, and so that I can give them the message."

We heard no more from brother John. He said he never wrote letters.

28.

Jesus Curses the Teachers of the Law and the Pharisees

(Matthew 23:1–36)

*The masters of the law and the Pharisees
have sat down in the chair of Moses.
Do and fulfill all that they say,
but do not follow their example,
because they say one thing and they do something else.*

"He says that because they were teaching
Scripture, and Scripture talks about love."

"There's nothing evil in the Bible, says
Jesus, because the whole message of the Bible
is freedom. The evil thing is that in teaching
the Bible some people, in practice, are defending the exploitation."

"Jesus distinguishes very well between doctrine and practice. He recommends the Bible
to us, but accompanied by revolutionary action."

"And the doctrine of the Bible isn't good for

291

anything unless it's practiced, right?"

I: "But it can be good for *us* if, as Christ says, we put into practice its freedom message that *they* didn't put into practice. Moses brought the people out of Egyptian slavery and took them to another land to found a kingdom of freedom, and the chair of Moses means the temple of freedom. Now just like then there are people in that temple preaching the Gospel and defending oppression. What they preach is false, but only because they don't practice it. If we put that into practice we change the world, we make a revolution."

For they pile on burdens so heavy that it is impossible to endure them,
and they make the people bear them,
but they don't want to touch them even with a finger.

OLIVIA: "It seems to me it's like when the priests preach to the poor that they must be content with their poverty. Like they used to preach to us here, when a priest would come once in a great while. They'd say that poverty was better than riches, because Christ chose poverty. With poverty you could get to heaven. Why did we want to have what the rich had? To live like we lived was what God wanted, and we ought to be happy with our lot. And they didn't live like that. They lived on board fancy yachts that some rich man lent them because they were friends of the rich. They piled a heavy burden on the people, the burden of misery, and they wouldn't even touch that misery with a ten-foot pole. And I suppose there are still priests like that in other places."

> *And they do everything so that people will look at them.*
> *On their foreheads and on their arms they like to wear parts of the Scripture written on wide bands*
> *and to put on clothes with longer fringes than other people.*

MANUEL: "Like the crosses that bishops go around with on their chests and the things they put on their heads and the garments of silk and lace and all that stuff."

GLORIA: "And going around with the Scriptures hanging on you reminds me of the Protestants that know the Bible by heart but they don't know how to love. They say that the Bible has nothing to do with politics. The poor have to be poor and the rich have to be rich and the exploiters exploit and the police kill and the bishops have no reason to interfere because they are ministers of Christ."

I: "Christ is talking about some adornments called phylacteries, short bits of Scripture attached to the sleeves and the forehead, because in one of the books of the Bible it says that the Scripture should always be kept 'close to the hand and in front of the eyes,' and they believed that by doing this they were complying."

WILLIAM: "You notice Jesus' scorn when he

describes those adornments. It's very ironic

294   *Matthew 23:1-36*

describes those adornments. It's very ironic when he talks to them about the pieces of Scripture used as adornments of their clothing to show off: what they attached to themselves were writings of the prophets denouncing their oppressions. And Jesus probably wasn't talking just for those people, he was talking also for the Christians that were going to go on doing the same thing in other ways."

They want to have the best places at meals
and the seats of honor in the synagogues,
and they want people to greet them with due
respect in the streets
and to call them teachers.

MARIITA: "And this thing that Christ attacked is still going on, because those church people are still at the head table at banquets and guests of honor at the big festivals and receptions and they like to be treated with great respect: Monsignor So-and-So."

Her mother: "In the Managua churches, which are like the synagogues, they say big Masses with three or four priests, wearing fancy capes. There they are, sitting in their seats, celebrating a very expensive Mass."

WILLIAM: "And you have to call them Reverend, Most Reverend, Most Illustrious, Your Excellency."

FELIPE: "And they think they're there to teach the people and that the people can't teach them anything and that the commentaries on the Scripture have to be made by them, because they are the teachers of the

law, the teachers of the Bible, and the people
are ignorant."

> *But you must not make the people call you*
> *teachers,*
> *because you are all brothers and sisters*
> *and you have only one Teacher, who is*
> *Christ.*

"We're all equal. The only teacher is Christ,
who is identified with the poor. The only
teacher we have is the people."

"He's condemning all class distinctions, and
having some people bossing other people."

I: "'Christ' is not a proper name; it's
the Greek word for Messiah, liberator. And
he's saying that we're all equal and that we
shouldn't have any teachers except the one
that brings those teachings about revolution."

WILLIAM: "It seems to me that 'teacher' was
a word that then meant something more than
it says now. It was a mainly religious word.
And I think he's alluding especially to those
'teachers of the law,' who were, so to speak,
owners of religion. And he's opposing the religious imposition of that kind of people."

TERESITA, his wife: "The only leader is
Christ, who brings no imposition except freedom."

> *And do not call any man on earth father,*
> *because you have one Father, the one who is*
> *in Heaven.*
> *Nor must you make people call you leaders,*
> *for Christ is the only leader.*

"That's just the same as Jesus said before. He condemns all paternalism. The father can also be the boss, the one you don't love but you respect him and you fear him like a father, and sometimes, if he's good, you're grateful to him like to a father."

"And there's another kind of father too, the leaders, who impose themselves by force, and we don't want to have that kind of father either."

I: "Leader or any other title is all the same. Here in Nicaragua the title that creates the greatest respect and fear is 'General.' "

"The Protestants don't call their ministers 'father,' because of what Jesus said. But it's not just a question of words. What he wants is to have no paternalism or tyranny of a leader, general, or anybody else."

"Not calling anybody leader is not saying like everybody says here in Nicaragua: 'the chief. . . .' The one that's screwing them is the chief."

ALEJANDRO: "Nobody should be chief, in the sense that nobody should have privileges, not in the sense that we shouldn't have leaders. That's why we shouldn't cling to one little word in the Gospel. The one that serves other people, the one that knocks himself out most, you might say, that one is the chief, and it's no problem to call him chief."

The one who serves others,
that one is the greatest among you.
For those who glorify themselves will be
*   humbled,*

> *but those who humble themselves will be*
> *glorified.*

WILLIAM: "That's why it seems to me very good to call the leaders the way they are called in Cuba: 'the responsible ones.' The responsible ones are those who take on a responsibility, who have a burden on their shoulders that the others don't have: the burden of all the rest of the people. The responsible ones are the ones that serve."

FELIPE: "The leaders don't become leaders because other people name them leaders, or because they name themselves, but through their own actions: because they serve the others."

ALEJANDRO: "And humbling yourself, like we said before, isn't making an ass of yourself."

TERESITA: "Humbling yourself is serving, and the opposite of serving others is to control others."

I: "The goal of the Gospel and the goal of communism is a society without a state and then we won't have teachers or a father or a chief. The people will be the only master and lord."

> *Woe to you, teachers of the law and Phar-*
> *isees, hypocrites, because you close the*
> *door of the kingdom of heaven*
> *so that others will not go in.*
> *You do not go in yourselves*
> *and you do not let others go in who want to go*
> *in.*

"The kingdom, as we all know, is that perfect society. He's telling them their religion is delaying the kingdom."

"It seems to me that it's because their children become other Pharisees right away, and they go on teaching others, each one another one, the older ones teaching the younger ones, and the children are going to become Pharisees later."

"It seems to me that he's telling them that because the Pharisees weren't able to be loving, and they couldn't teach other people to love. They don't love, and with their teaching they prevent love in other people," said FELIPE PEÑA.

ESPERANZA: "They don't want the new society for themselves and so they prevent the others from having it when they really want to have it."

I: "Religious alienation, according to Christ, prevents the people from getting freedom. He tells them that they are to blame for our still having the unjust society that we have. In other words, he tells them that they are an opiate of the people."

Woe to you teachers of the law and Pharisees,
     hypocrites,
because you rob widows of their homes
and to hide this you say long prayers.

"The widows are all the weak and unprotected. And here Jesus is talking to the capitalists. They do not only steal the widows' houses but their land too; and above all they steal the workers' work."

"If somebody has a little piece of land and things go bad for him, the bank takes it. And where does it wind up? With the capitalists. And they're often Christians and they go to Mass and say lots of prayers."

"And in those prayers they're asking God to steal more."

"And they go to their wealthy churches. They wouldn't come to this church because it has a dirt floor and it isn't a rich person's church."

I: "Reading what Jesus says here, you get the impression that not only was he against people that strip the poor. He was also against people that have a lot of religious practices. It seems he didn't sympathize much with those 'long prayers' he talked about when he talked about the thieves."

"There are other long prayers and they're political speeches. For example, the ones by Somoza."

WILLIAM: "Of course there's not just religious Phariseeism; nowadays what's more pernicious is political Phariseeism. Like the Phariseeism of the United States, that's shipping orphans out of Vietnam. After they destroyed Vietnam, they're saying long prayers before the world."

You travel over land and sea
to convert a person to your religion
and when you succeed you make that person

twice as deserving of hell as you are
yourselves.

"They convert him into a mess," said ALEJO.
"Maybe more of a gangster."
"The result of the evangelizing of an alien-
ated religion can be, for example, a Pinochet."

Woe unto you, blind guides! You say:
"Swearing by the temple doesn't count;
it's swearing by the gold in the temple that
counts."

"Even now the communion cups and the
chalices are more sacred than the people, who
are the temple of God."
"Or rather, in their religion the sacred thing
is gold. Or capital. According to Christ, the
temple, which is the person, is what makes
gold sacred. The human being is reality, and
Christ calls them blind guides because they're
like an opiate that makes people not see reality."
"They distinguished between the oath that
counts and the one that doesn't count; and the
teaching of Jesus is that nobody must be deceived, no matter what the oath is."

You give the tithe of mint, anise, and cumin
seed,
but you do not comply with the most impor-
tant thing in the law:
justice, mercy, and faith.

OLIVIA: "They gave the tithe of tiny little

plants but they had huge crops that were stolen because they got them by exploiting other people. Like those rich people that give a dime in church."

I said: "And here Jesus declares what is the most important thing about the law of the Bible. According to them it was the worship of God. According to Jesus it's justice, mercy, and faith. 'Justice' is the key word of the Bible, and we know what it is: it's the opposite of injustice, of oppression. Mercy in biblical language is the same as love or compassion: concretely it's to put yourself on the side of the poor, the orphans, the widows, the oppressed. So it's the equivalent of justice. And faith, in the Bible, is faith in justice. According to Jesus, then, the most important part of the Bible is justice, in the sense of social justice."

You strain at the mosquito, and you swallow the camel.

"There are still people very scrupulous in religious matters who pay a lot of attention to worship, to the decoration of churches, the communion cups, and all that, and they swallow the camels, which are injustice, exploitation. Those they swallow."

LAUREANO (whose family is evangelical): "People in the Church of the Nazarene swallow Somoza, the CIA, capitalism, the National Guard, but they don't smoke or drink."

You clean the outside of the glass and the dish,

but on the inside you are filled with what you
have achieved through theft and avarice.
Blind Pharisees:
first clean the glass and the dish on the in-
    side,
and then you will also be clean on the outside.

"They are apparently good people but they exploit others. They are good Christians crammed with stolen goods, because all their riches are stolen goods."

"To clean the dish on the inside would be to share whatever they have."

I: "They had many rites of purification, and it seems as though Jesus' image refers to that. But he doesn't tell them that their religious purification is only *external*, and that they must have an *internal* religious purification. He tells them that the real impurity is the appropriation of other people's work."

WILLIAM: "And since what they eat and drink is stolen, they first have to clean their dishes and their glasses of those thefts. And then they'll be all clean and they won't need any rite of purification."

"People who are in the mountains or in the underground, they've cleansed themselves on the inside; maybe they look dirty on the outside, but they're completely clean on the inside."

They are like whitewashed tombs that on the
    outside look so pretty
and on the inside are full of dead people's
    bones and all kinds of filth.

"Gentlemen that pay their workers five dollars a week and they seem so honorable and decent. They're scrubbed and well dressed and their hands are clean, their nails are clean, but they have stolen with those hands, and blood often runs from those hands."

"You look at their pretty, pretty houses, their bright polished cars, but in back of it all are all the filth of capitalism, prostitution, hunger, beggars, all kinds of corruption and death."

I said that, according to Jewish religious legalism, a corpse was 'impure.' With this image of the tombs Jesus is referring to the deep corruption hidden beneath their political, legal, and religious structure. This structure hasn't changed much from the system of slavery to the system of capitalism. It's just that now there's more decomposition, and now there's more stink.

You build the tombs of the prophets
and you adorn the monuments of people who
*   were good people*
and you say:
"If we had lived in the times of our ancestors
we would not have been accomplices in the
*   death of the prophets."*
You admit that you are the children of those
*   who killed the prophets.*
So finish up what your parents began!

I said I had read that in the time of Jesus many tombs were being built for the prophets that had been killed in the past. And Jesus notes a contradiction in the reactionaries: they erect tombs for martyrs and they kill martyrs. They kill the present martyrs and they erect tombs for the past ones. And it seems there's a relation between honor for the past and the murders of the present.

WILLIAM: "Reactionaries are people who respect a past revolution and oppose it to the present one. The reactionaries of the time of Christ worshipped the Scriptures of the prophets, who were great revolutionaries; and they even wore them on their clothes. And they were ready to kill Christ, the new prophet. And so today's reactionaries can worship the Christ of those times, but they kill today's Christ. And it's because today's reactionaries are children of yesterday's reactionaries, and they're all alike."

BOSCO: "They're a single chain. Reaction is a single thing across history. That's why Jesus says to those who want to kill him that they should finish what their ancestors began. In Nicaragua, in Chile, in many other places, they're still finishing that work."

EPILOGUE

In October 1977, during a period of countrywide up-heaval, the Nicaraguan National Guard ravaged the Solentiname community. In December, writing from Costa Rica, Cardenal explained in a "Letter to the People of Nicaragua" why he had joined the Sandinista guerrillas. The following translation by William Barbieri is reprinted with permission of the National Catholic Reporter, Box 281, Kansas City, MO 64141.

Twelve years ago I arrived at Solentiname with two companions to found a small, contemplative community. Contemplation means union with God. We soon became aware that this union with God brought us before all else into union with the peasants, very poor and very abandoned, who lived dispersed along the shores of the archipelago.

Contemplation also brought us to the revolution. It had to be that way. If not, it would have been fake contemplation. My old novice master, Thomas Merton, the inspirer and spiritual director of our foundation, told me that in Latin America I could not separate myself from political strife.

In the beginning we would have preferred a revolution with nonviolent methods. But we soon began to

305

realize that at this time in Nicaragua a nonviolent struggle is not feasible. Even Gandhi would agree with us. The truth is that all authentic revolutionaries prefer nonviolence to violence; but they are not always free to choose.

The Gospel was what most radicalized us politically. Every Sunday in Mass we discussed the Gospel in a dialogue with the peasants. With admirable simplicity and profound theology, they began to understand the core of the Gospel message: the announcement of the kingdom of God, that is, the establishment on this earth of a just society, without exploiters or exploited, with all goods in common, just like the society in which the first Christians lived. But above all else the Gospel taught us that the word of God is not only to be heard, but also to be put into practice.

As the peasants of Solentiname got deeper and deeper into the Gospel, they could not help but feel united to their brother and sister peasants who were suffering persecution and terror, who were imprisoned, tortured, murdered; they were violated and their homes were burnt. They also felt solidarity with all who with compassion for their neighbor were offering their lives. For this solidarity to be real, they had to lay security, and life, on the line.

In Solentiname it was well known that we were not going to enjoy peace and tranquillity if we wanted to put into practice the word of God. We knew that the hour of sacrifice was going to arrive. This hour has now come. Now in our community everything is over.

There a school of primitive painting became famous throughout the world. Paintings, woodwork, and various handicrafts from Solentiname are sold not only in Managua, but also in New York, Washington, Paris, Venezuela, Puerto Rico, Switzerland, and Germany. Lately peasants from Solentiname had begun to write beautiful poetry. Their poems were published in Nicaragua and other countries.

Several films were made in Solentiname, one of them by BBC in London. Much has been written about Solentiname in various languages; records have been made, even in German. We have in that distant corner of the lake a great library gathered during a lifetime. We had a collection of pre-Columbian art found in Solentiname that grew through the years. We had a large guest house with plenty of beds for visitors. We had ovens for ceramics and a large shop for all kinds of handicrafts. There we worked with wood, leather, copper, bronze, and silver. We were also developing communal work for young peasants through a cooperative. The cooperative, with the help of a German institution, was about ready to begin a dairy and factory of European-style cheese.

It was said in Germany: "Solentiname is everywhere, it is the beginning of a more human world. It is a Christian life—not just waiting for a better world, but working for their neighbor's peace, for peace in nature, for peace within the community." In Venezuela it was said that "Solentiname is something so God-like and so much of this world that it is a place where poetry, painting, and the harvest do not divide people into poets and farmers, but constitute the solidarity of one life." Now all that is over.

Twelve years ago, when the apostolic nuncio approved my project to found a new monastery, he told me that he would have preferred that the community be established in a less remote place than Solentiname, because there we would have no visitors. The truth is that we were always flooded with visitors from Nicaragua and other countries. Many times they were people who arrived in Nicaragua only to visit Solentiname; sometimes they arrived directly by way of Los Chiles or San Carlos, without any interest in even visiting Managua. Abundant correspondence from all parts of the world arrived in Solentiname.

But now brush will grow once again where our community used to be, just as it did before our arrival. There, there was a peasant mass, there were paintings, statues, books, records, classes, smiles of beautiful children, poetry, song. Now all that is left is the savage beauty of nature. I lived a very happy life in that near paradise that was Solentiname. But I was always ready to sacrifice it all. And now we have.

One day it happened that a group of boys and girls from Solentiname, because of profound convictions and after having let it mature for a long time, decided to take up arms. Why did they do it? They did it for only one reason: for their love for the kingdom of God, for the ardent desire that a just society be implanted, a real and concrete kingdom of God here on earth. When the time came, these boys and girls fought with great valor, but they also fought as Christians. That morning at San Carlos, they tried several times with a loudspeaker to reason with the guards so they might not have to fire a single shot. But the guards responded to their reasoning with submachine gunfire. With great regret, they also were forced to shoot.

Alejandro Guevara, one of those from my community, entered the building when in it there were no longer any but dead or wounded soldiers. He was going to set fire to it so that there would be no doubt about the success of the assault, but out of consideration for the wounded, he did not do it. Because the building was not burned, it was officially denied that it was taken. I congratulate myself that these young Christians fought without hate—above all, without hate for the wounded guards, poor peasants like themselves, also exploited. It is horrible that there are dead and wounded. We wish that there were not a struggle in Nicaragua, but this does not depend upon the oppressed people that are only defending themselves.

Some day there will be no more war in Nicaragua, no more peasant guards killing other peasants. Instead there will be an abundance of schools, hospitals, and clinics for everyone, food adequate for everyone, art and entertainment. But most important, there will be love among all.

Now the repression that has gone on so long in the North has arrived at Solentiname. A tremendous number of peasants have had to flee, others are in exile, remembering those beautiful islands with their now destroyed homes. They would be there yet, living tranquil lives, dedicated to their daily tasks. But they thought of their neighbor, and of Nicaragua, and began to work for them.

I do not think about the reconstruction of our small community of Solentiname. I think of a task much more important that we all have—the reconstruction of the whole country.

On July 19, 1979, the Sandinista revolution was victorious. Many of the Solentiname community participated in the struggle against the Somoza dictatorship. Ernesto Cardenal is now Minister of Culture of Nicaragua.